The Practice of the

PRESENCE OF GOD

by

BROTHER LAWRENCE OF THE
RESURRECTION

Translated by

SISTER MARY DAVID, S.S.N.D.

Paulist Press
New York, N.Y./Ramsey, N.J.

First published by the Newman Press, Westminster, Maryland in 1945. Revised edition published by Paulist Press, New York, N.Y., 1978.

Preface Copyright © 1978
by The Missionary Society
of St. Paul the Apostle
in the State of New York

ISBN: 0-8091-2137-9
Library of Congress
Catalog Card number: 78-61665

Published by
Paulist Press
Editorial office: 1865 Broadway, New York, N.Y. 10023
Business office: 545 Island Road, Ramsey, N.J. 07446

Printed and bound in the
United States of America

Preface

BY ANNE FREMANTLE

WHAT has a lay brother who died aged eighty in an obscure monastery in Europe on 12 February 1691 to say to us today? The biographical facts in his long life are few. Nicolas Herman was born of pious peasant parents in Lorraine. Aged eighteen, looking at a tree in winter, bare of leaves, and realising that "some time later the leaves would appear again, then flowers, then fruits" he received "a profound impression of the providence and the power of God, which was never effaced from his soul". He first became a soldier, like Joan of Arc, who came from the same part of the world, Francis of Assisi, and Ignatius Loyola. Nicolas was captured by Germans, who thought he was a spy and threatened to hang him. But he told them "he was not what they supposed" and "as his conscience did not reproach him with any crime, he looked upon death with indifference. At that, the officers released him". Next, he was wounded, by Swedes making an incursion into Lorraine. During his convalescence, like Francis and Ignatius, he decided to "abandon the profession of arms." He had an uncle who was a "holy Discalced Carmelite religious" and Nicolas applied to become a lay brother in the same monastery. Not finding "peace of mind" in the religious life, he suffered ten years from "fear and anxiety" believing certainly that "he was damned". For four of those years the anguish was so great "that all the men in the world could never have taken out of his mind the thought that he would be damned". All this time he had "no comfort in prayer, no lessening of his pain". But he reasoned, he tells us, in this way: "I came into religion only for the love of God, I have tried to act only for Him. Whether I be damned or saved, I wish to continue to act purely for the love of God". Then suddenly Brother Lawrence, as he had become, "perceived a ray of divine light which, illuminating his spirit, dissipated all his fears, and ended his pain". For the next forty years, until his death, he lived in that light. From that time on he "no longer thought of heaven nor hell, nor of his past sins, nor of those he was committing, after he had asked pardon of God for them."

At first he worked in the monastery kitchen, for which work he had, he said, "the greatest natural aversion". But he did "alone the work that two people usually do and was never seen to bustle". He said "I turn my little omelette in the pan for the love of God" and would not "pick a straw up from the floor except for the love of God". He had been a "clumsy fellow" as he described himself. Even before he became a lay brother, when he was a "lackey" he used to break everything. Later, when his monastery sent him into Burgundy to buy wine he could not walk "on the boat without rolling against the barrels". But he did not "worry about his awkwardness any more than about his whole purchase of wine". He simply told God "that it was His affair" after which "everything turned out nicely". Brother Lawrence was lame, perhaps from his wounds but certainly from sciatica. He began to suffer from a huge ulcer on his leg, and was set to repairing shoes, a job "he liked very much". He found God there "as much as when he was praying with the community".

He declared that unnecessary thoughts "spoil everything", and that instead of indulging in them "one should practice the presence of God in one single act that does not end". His soul was "always in the ceaseless exercise of the Divine presence. But he warned that "one does not become holy all of a sudden". Yet "time presses and there is no reprieve". Though he felt "no anxiety nor doubt" about his state, he insisted that "we must watch carefully over all the movements of the soul". He himself had "no memory of things he did—upon rising from the table he did not know what he had eaten. "The heart must be emptied of everything else" yet "God must be served with holy freedom". It is the view "we take of trials that make them seem unbearable". As long as love is great "we will love equally in distress and consolation". To those who would consider this state as laziness, deception, self-love" he replied "I declare that it is a holy laziness and a blessed self-love".

What is there in this simple, edifying, remote life for us? It may seem paradoxical that what Brother Lawrence has to say to us above all is *never mind*: never mind how clumsy you are, or how stupid, or how sinful; never mind what results you achieve; never mind whether you get to heaven or hell. This Brother Lawrence teaches us by his total indifference to the "fruit of action".

Brother Lawrence was, of course, just as indifferent to his own spiritual welfare as to his worldly success or failure. If there were no heaven or hell, he said, it would make no difference to him, echoing Rabia al Adawiyya's (d. 801) prayer: "If I love Thee from fear of hell, send me to hell; if I love Thee from hope of heaven, keep me from heaven. But if I love Thee for Thyself, let me come to Thee".

And as the great Jewish mystic Hillel put it: "If not here, where? If not now, when?" Brother Lawrence tells us that we must practice being in the presence of God here, and now.

Contents

A Eulogy of Brother Lawrence

BY M. L'ABBÉ JOSEPH DE BEAUFORT

IT IS a truth constantly recurring in Holy Scripture that the arm of God is not shortened, since His mercy cannot be exhausted by our miseries. The power of His grace is no less great today than it was in the first days of the Church. As He wished to perpetuate for Himself until the end of the world saints who would render Him a homage worthy of His grandeur and majesty, and who by the holiness of their example would be models of virtue, He did not content Himself with causing the birth, in the early centuries, of extraordinary men, who would acquit themselves properly of this double obligation; but He still raises up, from time to time, men who perfectly fulfill these two duties and who guard in themselves the first fruits of the spirit, transmit them and make them live again in others.

Such a man is Brother Lawrence of the Resurrection, a discalced Carmelite lay-brother, whom God caused to be born in these latter days to render Him all the homage due to Him and to animate the

Brothers by the rare example of his piety to the practice of all virtues.

He was named in the world Nicholas Herman. His father and his mother, upright people who led an exemplary life, inspired in him the fear of God in his childhood and took particular pains with his education, setting before him only principles that are holy and consistent with the Gospel.

Lorraine, which witnessed his birth at Hérimini, having involved him in its unhappy affairs, he embraced the profession of arms, in which, conducting himself with simplicity and honesty, he received from God evidence of His goodness and His mercy.

Having been made a prisoner by a small body of German troops, he was treated as a spy. Who could imagine how far his patience and his calmness went in this disagreeable event? They threatened to hang him. But he, without becoming terrified, answered that he was not what they supposed; and besides, since his conscience did not reproach him with any crime, he looked upon death with indifference. At that, the officers released him.

When the Swedes made an expedition into Lorraine and attacked in passing the little town of Rambervilliers, our young soldier was wounded there, and his injury forced him to retire to the home of his parents, who were not far away.

This adventure gave him the occasion of abandoning the profession of arms to undertake a more holy one, and to fight under the standard of Jesus Christ. No vain transports of indiscreet zeal disgusted him with so tumultuous a state; it was through sentiments of true devotion that he resolved to give himself wholly to God and to repair his past conduct. This God of all consolation who was destining him for a more holy life then made him perceive the nothingness of the vanities of the world, touched him with the love of heavenly things. But these first impressions of grace did not at once accomplish their full effect. He reflected often upon the perils of his profession, the vanity and the corruption of the century, the instability of men, the treason of an enemy, the infidelity of his friends; and it was only after lively considerations, rude interior struggles, tears and sighs that, conquered at last by the strength of the eternal truths, he took a firm resolution to attach himself finally to the practices of the Gospel and to walk in the footprints of a holy discalced Carmelite religious who was his uncle. This man had made him realize that the air of the world is contagious and that, if it does not strike with death those who breathe it, at least it spoils or corrupts the manners of those who follow its principles.

The wise advice of this enlightened director made the way of perfection easy for Herman. To this end, too, the fine dispositions of his soul contributed not a little. The common sense, the prudence which were evident even upon his countenance, soon freed him from all the difficulties that the world and the devil ordinarily oppose to those who wish to change their lives. That prudent firmness which was so natural to him gave him such generous determination for this that he was raised up in a moment and as if by a miracle.

It was in meditating upon the promises of his baptism, the disorders of his youth, the mysteries of our Christian faith and above all the passion of Jesus Christ—of which he never thought without being sensibly moved—that he was changed into another man, and the humility of the cross appeared to him fairer than all the glory of the world.

Thus fired with a fervor wholly divine, he sought for God according to the advice of the Apostle, in the simplicity and the sincerity of his heart. He desired only solitude, in order to weep for his sins; and being sufficiently mature in age to feel sure of his resolve, he thought more than once of retirement. A favorable occasion came, as I am about to relate.

There was a gentleman to whom noble birth and valor offered a bright future, but who, being little satisfied with himself, always uneasy in the midst of his wealth and convinced that God alone could fill the extent of his desires, had preferred evangelical poverty to all the treasures of earth. Since he had cast himself into a hermitage to taste how sweet the Lord is to them that seek him in truth, our Herman profited by so lucky a circumstance. His soul, weary at last of the painful life it was leading, began to desire repose. Accompanied by so faithful a guide, he had no difficulty in retiring into the desert, where the Christian strength with which he was animated dissipated his fears and where he attached himself to God more than ever.

But, although the eremitical life is excellent for the advanced and the perfect, it is not ordinarily the best for beginners; this our new solitary perceived clearly. Seeing joy, sadness, peace, anxiety, fervor and tepidity, confidence and heaviness, rule by turns in his soul, he doubted the wisdom of his course; and he wished to enter a congregation in order to embrace within it a type of life whose rule, founded not on the shifting sands of temporary devotion but on the firm rock of Jesus Christ—Who is the base of all religious practices—would secure him against the changeableness of his whims.

Terrified nevertheless at the prospect of perpetual vows and perhaps tempted by the devil, he could not take this step. Day after day he grew more irresolute until, having listened once again to God, Who was calling him with so many caresses, he came to Paris to ask for the religious habit, received it among the lay-brothers of the Order of Discalced Carmelites, and was named Brother Lawrence of the Resurrection.

From the very beginning of his novitiate, he applied himself with much fervor to the exercises of the religious life. His devotion to the Blessed Virgin was extraordinary. He was tenderly devoted to her; he had a filial confidence in her protection; she was his refuge in all the vicissitudes of his life, in the trouble and anxiety with which his soul was agitated; he called her habitually his good Mother. He gave himself particularly to the practice of prayer. However great his occupations were, they never made him lose the time destined for this holy exercise. Recollection of the presence of God and the love which are its effects were his dearest virtues: they made him in a short time the model of his fellow-novices; and the conquering grace of Jesus Christ made him embrace with ardor the penance and seek out the mortifications that nature flees with so much aversion.

Although the superiors assigned Lawrence to the humblest duties, he never made any complaint; on the contrary, grace, which does not recoil from what is harsh and rude, sustained him in employment in which everything is unpleasant and tiresome. Whatever repugnance he felt on the side of nature, he accepted these duties with pleasure, deeming himself too fortunate, either to suffer or to be humiliated according to the example of the Saviour. The conviction people had of his worth and the esteem that he had acquired by his heroic acts of virtue obliged the master of novices, in order to test his vocation and the firmness of his purpose, to heap up difficulties and to try him with different duties and sharply to rebuke him; but he, far from being discouraged at this test, sustained it with the fidelity that was to be expected. This appeared again upon another occasion when, a religious having come to tell him that they were talking of dismissing him from the monastery, he replied: "I am in the hands of God; He will do with me as He pleases. I do not act through human respect. If I do not serve Him here, I will serve Him elsewhere."

The time of his profession having arrived, he did not hesitate at all to sacrifice himself to God, without reserve. I could here recall several fine deeds that would convince the reader of the completeness of his sacrifice and that would deserve special attention; but I pass over them in silence in order to expatiate more upon the interior sufferings with which his soul was afflicted—partly by an order of Divine Providence which permitted this to purify him, and partly also through lack of experience, as he tried to move in his own fashion in the spiritual life. He remembered the sins of his past life, and this sight caused him horror, rendering him so slight and contemptible in his own eyes that he judged himself unworthy of the least caresses of the Bridegroom; yet he perceived himself to be extraordinarily favored, and in the humble feeling that he had of his own misery, he dared not accept the heavenly gifts that were presented to him, not yet knowing that God would be so merciful as to communicate Himself to a sinner such as he believed himself to be. It was then that the fear of illusion began to take possession of his heart and that his state appeared to him so dubious that he no longer knew what to do—which caused him such terrible torments that the only way he could express them was to compare them to those of hell.

In this distressing state, he used to go often into a retired spot close to his little den, where there was a picture of the Saviour bound to the pillar. There, his heart afflicted, all bathed in tears, he would pour out his troubles to God and conjure Him not to let him perish, since he placed all his trust in Him and had no other intention than to please Him.

However, no matter how he prayed to God, his troubles did not cease to be increased by fears and perplexities so embarrassing that his soul was suddenly stopped. Solitude, which he had regarded as a safe harbor, then seemed to him like a sea agitated with furious tempests. His frightened spirit, like a vessel beaten by winds and storm, abandoned by its pilot, knew not what course to take nor what resolution to make; for on one side he felt a secret inclination which impelled him to give himself to the Lord by a continual immolation of himself, and on the other hand, the fear that he had of departing from the ordinary way made him innocently resist God. Everything trying to nature that he visualized filled him with horror, and it all appeared frightful to him. Besides, his soul was plunged into such bitterness and such thick darkness that neither from heaven nor from earth did he receive any help.

This line of action, rigorous though it may be, is nevertheless the one that God often employs in order to test the virtue of His true servants, before confiding to them the inestimable treasures of His wisdom; and it is the course He used in regard to Brother Lawrence.

One cannot imagine how great were his patience, his gentleness, his temperance, his firmness and his tranquillity in these trials. As he was humble in his thoughts and his conduct, having only a slight opinion of himself, he really valued nothing but suffering and humiliation. Moreover, he asked only for the chalice of the Lord and he was made to drink all its bitterness.

If only God had pleased to preserve for him a little of the consolation he had felt at the beginning of his penitence! But no; it was all taken away. Ten years of fear and anxiety gave him very little respite: no comfort in prayer, no lessening of his pain. That was what made life so difficult for him and reduced him to so extreme a want that he became a burden to himself and could not endure himself. Faith alone was his support.

In this turmoil of different thoughts that reduced him to extremity, his courage did not fail him. On the contrary, in his worst troubles he always had recourse to prayer, to the exercise of the presence of God, to the practice of all the

Christian and religious virtues, to corporal austerities, to groans and tears, to long vigils. Sometimes he passed almost entire nights or a whole day before the Most Blessed Sacrament, reflecting upon the troubles with which his soul was afflicted; and knowing that it was for the love of God and through fear of displeasing Him that he suffered them, he made a generous resolution to endure them not only the rest of his life but even for all eternity, if it so pleased God: "For," he said, "it no longer matters to me what I do or what I suffer, provided that I remain lovingly united to His will, since that is my whole concern."

This was precisely the disposition in which God wished him to be, in order to overwhelm him with His graces. So, from that moment on, the firmness of his soul grew greater than ever; and God, Who needs neither time nor much reasoning to make Himself heard, suddenly opened his eyes. Lawrence perceived a ray of divine light which, illuminating his spirit, dissipated all his fears, ended his pain; and the graces that he received recompensed him well for all his past afflictions. It was then that he experienced what the great Saint Gregory says, that the world appears very small to a soul that contemplates the grandeur of God. His letters addressed to a Carmelite Sister do not permit any doubt of it, and here in a few words is what they contain:

> The whole world no longer seems able to stay with me. Everything that I see with my bodily eyes passes before me like phantoms and dreams; what I see with the eyes of the soul is alone what I desire—and to find myself still a little separated from it is the cause of my listlessness and torment. Dazzled on one side by the brilliance of this divine Sun of justice That dissipates the shadows of the night, and blinded on the other hand by the mud of my misery, I am often almost beside myself. However, my usual practice is to remain in the presence of God with all the humility of a useless but faithful servant.

This holy exercise molded his individual character. The habit of it that he had formed was so natural to him that, as he has himself explained in some one of his letters and in what he has written about it elsewhere, he passed the last forty years of his life in a constant exercise of the presence of God—or rather, to use his own words, in a mute, familiar conversation with Him.

A monk whose question he could not avoid having asked him one day what means he had used to acquire this custom of the presence of God, the exercise of which was so easy and so continuous for him, he replied with his habitual simplicity:

From the moment of my entrance into religion, I looked upon God as the limit and the end of all the thoughts and affections of my soul. At the beginning of my novitiate, during the hours designated for prayer I occupied myself in convincing myself of the truth of this Divine Being, rather by the light of faith than by the labor of meditation and reading; and by this short and sure means I advanced in the knowledge of this lovable Person, with whom I resolved to dwell always. Then, wholly penetrated as I was with the grandeur of this infinite Being, I used to shut myself up in the place that obedience had destined for me, which was the kitchen. There, alone, after having arranged all the things necessary for my duty, I used to devote to prayer all the time that was left, as much before my work as after it. At the beginning of my duties I would say to God with filial confidence, "My God, since Thou art with me and since by Thine order I must occupy my mind with these external things, I beg Thee to grant me the grace to remain with Thee and to keep Thee company; but that it may be the better done, my Lord, work with me, receive my labors and possess all my affections." Then, during my work, I continued to speak to Him familiarly, to offer Him my little services and to ask His graces. At the end of the action, I used to examine how I had done it. If I found good in it, I thanked God. If I noticed faults, I asked His pardon for them and without being discouraged I purified my intention and began again to dwell with God as if I had not strayed from Him. Thus, rising up after my falls and making a multiplicity of acts of faith and of love, I have arrived at a state in which it would be as impossible for me not to think of

God as it was difficult for me to accustom myself to it in the beginning.

As he was experiencing the great profit that this holy exercise brings to the soul, he advised all his friends to apply themselves to it with all the care and fidelity that they could. To make them undertake it with firm resolution and invincible courage, he gave them such strong and efficacious reasons that he not only persuaded their minds but even penetrated their hearts and made them love and undertake this holy practice with as much fervor as they had previously regarded it with indifference. If he had the gift of persuading by his speech those who approached him, he did so no less by his good example. One had only to look at him to be edified and to put oneself in the presence of God, no matter how rushed one might be.

He called the exercise of the presence of God the shortest and easiest way to arrive at Christian perfection, the mold and the life of virtue and the great preservative from sin.

He declared that to make this practice easy and to form the habit of it, one needed only courage and good will: a truth that he demonstrated far better by his works than by his words. For it was evident in his deportment, when he was busy in the kitchen, that underneath his continuous work and in the midst of the most distracting occupations he kept his spirit recollected in God. Although his duties were great and hard, since he often did alone the work that two people usually do, he was never seen to bustle; but with a just moderation he gave to each duty the time that it required, always preserving his modest and tranquil air, working neither slowly nor swiftly, dwelling in calmness of soul and unalterable peace.

He performed this duty with all possible charity for about thirty years, until Providence ordained otherwise. A big ulcer came upon his leg, which obliged the superiors to employ him at an easier task. This change gave him more leisure to adore God in spirit and in truth, as was his disposition, and to occupy himself more perfectly with His pure presence by the exercise of faith and of love.

In this intimate union—which can result only from these two virtues—the species of creatures, of which one can rid oneself only with difficulty, were effaced from his imagination; the powers of hell, which never grow weary of attacking men, no longer dared to molest Lawrence; his passions grew so calm that he scarcely felt them any more, or, if sometimes to humiliate him they excited a little emotion, he then resembled those high mountains that see meteors formed only at their feet.

From that time on, he seemed to have a character made only for virtue: a gentle disposition, entire honesty and the best heart in the world. His kind face, his gracious and affable air, his simple and modest manner, at once won him the esteem and the good will of all who saw him. The more familiar with him they grew, the more they discovered in him a fund of uprightness and of piety such as is hardly found elsewhere.

It has been remarked that, since it had been one of his cares not to show any singularity in his conduct, he always preserved the simplicity of the common life, without putting on that melancholy, austere air that serves only to rebuff people. He, who was not one of that sort who never bend and who regard sanctity as incompatible with normal customs, who had no affectations, fraternized with everyone and moved kindly among his brothers and his friends, without trying to be distinguished from them.

Very far from presuming on the graces of God and from parading his virtues in order to win esteem, he tried assiduously to lead a hidden and unknown life. Just as a proud man exerts himself to seek out all imaginable means to procure an advantageous place in men's opinion, so one can say that the man who is truly humble bends every effort not only to avoid the applause and the praise of creatures, but even to destroy the good opinion of him that they may have. In ancient times there were saints who purposely did ridiculous things in order to draw down upon themselves the contempt and the mockery of everyone, or at least to inspire doubts of the high opinion of their merit that had been conceived. It was thus that Brother Lawrence acted. His humility, which I may call his special characteristic, sometimes made him find holy devices and apparent childishness, to conceal his virtue and hide its splendor. He was not seeking the glory of humility, but its reality; and as he did not wish to have anyone but God for witness of his acts, neither did he propose to himself any other reward but God.

Although he was so reserved about himself, he did not fail to communicate his ideas, for the edification of his brothers, not to the most enlightened—whose knowledge and inspirations often swell the heart—but to little ones and the simplest; it was observed that when he found some of this stamp, he had no secrets from them. He disclosed to them with wonderful simplicity the fairest secrets of the interior life and the treasures of divine wisdom. The sweetness that accompanied his words so charmed those who had the advantage of conversing with him that they came away penetrated with the love of God and burning with the desire to put into execution the great truths that he had just taught them in secret.

As God was leading him more by love than by the fear of His judgment, so all his conferences tended to inspire this same love, to break the slightest attachments to creatures and to cause the death of the old man, so as to establish the reign of the new. "If you wish to make great progress in the spiritual life," he used to tell his brothers, "pay no attention to the fine words nor the elegant discourses of the learned of this world. Bad luck to those who try to satisfy their curiosity with the learning of men! It is the Creator Who teaches truth, Who in one moment instructs the heart of the humble and makes him understand more about the mysteries of our Faith and even about the Godhead than if he had studied them for a long term of years."

It was for this reason that he carefully avoided answering those curious questions which lead nowhere, which serve only to burden the spirit and dry up the heart. But when his superiors obliged him to declare his thoughts upon the difficulties that were proposed in conferences, his answers were so clear and to the point that they needed no comment. That is what many learned men, both diocesan and religious clergymen, remarked when they obliged him to reply to them.

That was also the judicial opinion that a certain illustrious bishop of France formed in the interviews that he had with Brother Lawrence, which obliged him to say in his favor that he had rendered himself worthy to have God speak to him interiorly and discover to him His mysteries. He added that the greatness and the purity of his love for God made him live on the earth as if he were already one of the blessed.

He raised his soul to God through the knowledge of created things, convinced as he was that the books of the most famous academies teach very little in comparison with the great book of the world, when one knows how to study it properly. His soul, moved by the diversity of the different parts of creation, raised itself to God so powerfully that nothing could separate it from Him. He observed in each of its wonders the different characteristics of the power, the wisdom and the goodness of the Creator, which ravished his spirit with admiration and raised his heart in transports of love and joy, so that he cried out with the Prophet: "O Lord, God of gods, how incompre-

hensible art Thou in Thy thoughts, how profound
in Thy designs, how powerful in all Thine actions."

He wrote such lofty and tender phrases, as much
upon the grandeur of God as upon the ineffable
communications of His love with souls, that those
who have seen a few scattered pages of these writ-
ings (which he lent only reluctantly and upon
the condition of their speedy return) were so
charmed and edified that they spoke of them only
with admiration. No matter how much trouble he
took to hide them, this precision has not prevented
the survival of some fragments, which make us
regret the rest; for, if we may judge all he did by
the little of his letters and his maxims that remains
to us, there is every reason to believe what he declared to one of his friends—that his little compo-
sitions were actually effusions of the Holy Spirit
and products of His love. Sometimes Brother Lawrence expressed them on paper, but comparing
what he had just written with what he felt interiorly, he judged it so inferior and so far from
the high conception he had of the grandeur and
the goodness of God that he often found himself
obliged to tear it up immediately. He tore it up
with the more good will because he had written it
only to relieve himself of his fullness, to let his
spirit soar and to expand his heart and his breast,

which were too narrow to contain the divine fire
that devoured him. It made him suffer strangely,
like a fountain which, unable to hold its waters,
has to spread them abroad; or like a subterranean
place that, powerless to arrest the violence of the
fire within, must give it issue and passage.

Among the virtues which excelled in Brother
Lawrence, one of the principal ones was faith.
As the just man lives by this theological virtue,
it was the life and the nourishment of his soul. It
gave such increase to his soul that he visibly made
progress in the interior life. This fair virtue it
was which had set the whole world beneath his
feet and rendered it so contemptible in his eyes
that he thought it unworthy to occupy the smallest space in his heart. It was faith which led him
to God and, elevating him above all created things,
made him seek happiness in the possession of Him
alone. It was his great instructor; faith alone taught
him more than the reading of all books.

It was faith that gave him that high esteem for
God, that great reverence for the sacred mysteries,
especially for the Most Blessed Sacrament of the
altar, in which the Son of God resides like a King.
To Him he was so devoted that he passed many
hours, day and night, at His feet to render Him
homage and adoration. This same faith gave him

a profound respect for the word of God, for the Church and its holy precepts, for his superiors, whom he obeyed as the vicars of Jesus Christ. Finally, with such conviction did he believe the truth that faith proposes to us, that he often used to say:

> All the fine speeches that I hear about God, what I can myself read about Him or feel about Him, would not be enough to satisfy me; for, being infinite in His perfections, He is consequently ineffable, and there are no words eloquent enough to give me a perfect conception of His grandeur. It is faith that discovers them to me and makes me know Him as He is. By means of it I learn more about Him in a short time than I would learn in many years in the schools.

Crying out, he said: "O faith, faith, admirable virtue! You enlighten the mind of man and conduct him to the knowledge of his Creator. Lovable virtue, how little you are known and still less practised, although the knowledge of you is so glorious and so profitable."

Of this lively faith were born the firmness of his hope in the goodness of God, a filial confidence in His providence, a total and universal abandonment of himself into His hands, without worrying what would become of him after his death— as we will be able to see more fully, when we speak of the sentiments he entertained in his last illness. He was not content, during the greater part of his life, with entrusting his salvation to the power of grace and the merits of Jesus Christ; but forgetting himself and all his own interests, he threw himself, as the Prophet says, recklessly into the arms of infinite mercy. The more desperate things appeared to him, the more he hoped—like a rock beaten by the waves of the sea and settling itself more firmly in the midst of the tempest—as we have already noticed in the interior trials that God sent him soon after his entrance into religion, to test his fidelity. If, in the words of Saint Augustine, the measure of hope is the measure of grace, what shall we say of that which God gave to Brother Lawrence, to him who, as Scripture says, hoped against hope? That is why he said that the greatest glory one can give to God is to mistrust his own strength entirely and to confide himself completely to His protection; because in that way one makes a sincere avowal of one's own weakness and a true confession of the omnipotence of the Creator.

As charity is the queen and the soul of all the virtues, which necessarily gives them worth and value, we need not wonder that those which Brother Lawrence possessed were perfect, since the love of God reigned so completely in his heart that he had turned all his affections, as Saint Bernard says, toward this divine Object. If faith made him regard God as sovereign truth, and if hope made him think of Him as his last end and his complete happiness, charity caused him to conceive of Him as the most perfect of all beings, or, to speak better, as perfection itself.

Far from loving God in return for His benefits, He had so disinterested a charity that he would have loved God even though there had been no punishment to avoid nor any reward to attain, desiring only the good and the glory of God and forming his Heaven of the accomplishment of His holy will. This was especially evident in the extremity of his final illness, in which even to his last breath his spirit was so free that he expressed the sentiments of his heart as if he had been in perfect health.

The purity of his love was so great that he would have wished, if it had been possible, that God should not know the actions he did for His service, so that he might do them solely for His glory and without self-interest. However, he complained lovingly and used to tell his friends that God did not let any of them pass without immediately rewarding him a hundredfold, often giving him delights and sensations of His divinity that were overwhelming. These experiences constrained him to say, with his usual familiarity:

It is too much, O Lord! It is too much for me. Give, if it please Thee, these kinds of favors and consolations to sinners and to the people who do not know Thee, in order to attract them to Thy service. As for me, who have the happiness of knowing Thee by faith, I think that must be sufficient; but because I ought not refuse anything from a hand so rich and generous as Thine, I accept, O my God, the favors Thou givest me. Yet grant, if it please Thee, that after having received them, I may return them just as Thou didst give them to me; for Thou knowest well that it is not Thy gifts that I seek and desire, but Thyself, and I can be content with nothing less.

This purity of love and this disinterestedness served only to fire his heart the more and to increase the flames of this divine conflagration, from which the sparks sometimes flew outside. For although he used all his efforts to hide the great surges of divine love that burned within him, it was not always in his power to check its outbursts; and he was often seen, against his will, with his countenance all radiant. But when he was in privacy, he let the fullness of the fire glow and cried to God: "O Lord, give more space and issue to the faculties of my soul, so that I may give room to

Thy love; or, rather, sustain me by Thine almighty strength, for otherwise I shall be consumed by the flames of Thy love."

He often used to say to God—in the conversation that he had with his Brothers, regretting the time he had lost in his youth:

> O Goodness, so ancient and so new, too late have I loved Thee! Do not act this way, my Brothers. You are young; profit by the sincere confession I make to you of the little care I took to consecrate my first years to God. Consecrate all of yours to His love; for, as for me, if I had known sooner and if anyone had told me, the things that I am telling you now, I would not have waited so long to love Him. Believe me, and count for lost all the time that is not spent in loving God.

Since the love of God and the love of neighbor are but one same custom, judge of his charity towards his neighbor by that which he had for God, persuaded that it is of the kind Our Lord describes in the Gospel: that the least service rendered to the smallest of his Brothers, he counts as done to himself. Brother Lawrence took particular care to serve them in all the offices he filled, especially when he was employed in the kitchen. Foreseeing all that was needed for the nourishment of the religious, conformably to their poverty, he took his pleasure in contenting them as if they had been angels—a charity that he inspired in all those who have succeeded him in this duty.

He assisted the poor in their needs, as much as was in his power. He consoled them in their afflictions; he aided them with his advice, he urged them to earn Heaven at the same time that they were working to earn their living; and, to sum it up in a few words, he did to his neighbor all the good he could and never any harm to anyone. He made himself all things to all men, to win them all for God.

As, in the phrase of Saint Paul, charity is patient, triumphs over all difficulties and suffers everything for the one it loves, can one doubt the patience of Brother Lawrence in his infirmities, the patience of him who loved God very perfectly? Indeed, if in the thought of the same Apostle, patience has this fine relationship with charity—that, as the latter is the bond of perfection, the former is a perfect work, *opus perfectum habet*—do we need more to convince us of the perfect state to which God raised Brother Lawrence? That is what we shall see in the practice of these two virtues, in the midst of the very painful maladies with which God was pleased to afflict him. Without mentioning here a sort of sciatica that made him lame, which tormented him about twenty-five years and, having degenerated into an ulcer on the leg, caused him acute pain, I will dwell chiefly upon three heavy illnesses that God sent him in the last years of his life, to prepare him for death and to render him worthy of the reward that He destined for him.

The two first ones reduced him to extremity; but he endured them with admirable patience and kept in the midst of his sufferings the same serenity of soul that he had had in the most vigorous health. In the first one, he displayed some desire of death when, speaking to the doctor and feeling his fever grow less, he said, "Oh, sir, your remedies succeed too well for me; you are only retarding my happiness!" In the second, he appeared to have no inclination. He remained in entire indifference about life or death, perfectly resigned to the decrees of God and as content to live as to die. He wanted only what it might please Divine Providence to ordain.

But in the third sickness, which separated his soul from his body to unite it in heaven with his Beloved, I can say that he displayed marks of a constancy, a resignation and a joy that were quite extraordinary. As for a long time he had been sighing after this blessed moment, when he saw that it had arrived he felt profound satisfaction. The sight of death, which terrifies men and casts the boldest into consternation, did not frighten him at all. He gazed upon it with a calm eye. One might almost say he defied it, for, having seen the poor couch that had been prepared for him and having heard one of his friends say: "It is all over with you, Brother Lawrence; you'll have to go," he answered, "That is so. This is my deathbed. But very soon one who does not expect to will follow me." This did indeed happen as he had predicted; for, although this Brother was in perfect health, he fell ill the next day and died the same day as Brother Lawrence was buried and on the next Wednesday was interred in the same grave. It seems that the charity which had united these two good Brothers during life did not want them to be separated in death, since at that time there was no other grave but this one in the community cemetery.

Four or five months had passed since Brother Lawrence had told several persons that he would die before the end of February. He wrote two letters, two weeks apart, to a Sister of the Blessed Sacrament. Finishing the first, he said, "Goodbye. I hope to see Him soon." The second, dated February sixth, two days before he fell ill, he ended with these words: "Farewell. I hope from His mercy the grace to see Him in a few days."

The very day that he was confined to bed, he

said to one of his confidants among the religious
that his illness would not be long and that he would
leave the world as soon as possible. He was so sure
of the day of his death that on the morrow—which
was Friday—he spoke more precisely and told a
Brother that he would die the following Monday.
This happened as he had said.

But let us return to the constancy that he displayed in his sickness, before remarking the circumstances of his death and the last sentiments
that he had in his extremity. The only desire that
remained to him was to suffer something for the
love of God. This made him reiterate what he had
said many times in his life: that he had only one
pain, which was that he did not have any, *and
that he consoled himself by reflecting that there
is a purgatory and that there, at least, he would
suffer something in reparation for his sins.* But,
having found a favorable occasion for it in this
life, he did not let it escape. He purposely had
himself turned on the right side; and as he knew
that this position was extremely painful for him,
he wished to remain in it to content the eager
desire he had for suffering. A Brother who watched
beside him wanted to relieve him a little; but he
answered, twice: "Thank you, Brother. I beg you,
let me suffer a little for the love of God." In this

painful state, he said fervently: "My God, I adore Thee in my infirmities. Right now, O my God, I will suffer something for Thee. Be it so: let me suffer and die with Thee." Then he repeated often these verses from the fiftieth Psalm: "Create a clean heart within me, O God. . . . Cast me not away from thy face. . . . Restore unto me the joy of thy salvation. . . ."

The pains that he felt in this position, because of a stitch in the right side caused by pleurisy, were so acute that he would unquestionably have died if the infirmarian, arriving at the opportune moment and perceiving this, had not promptly changed him to the other side and so let him breathe freely. He was so enamoured of suffering that it constituted his entire consolation. He never appeared to have a moment's sorrow in the greatest access of his sickness. His joy was evident not only upon his countenance, but even in his manner of speaking—which caused some religious who were visiting him to ask whether he were really not suffering at all.

"Excuse me," he said. "I am in pain; this stitch in my side hurts, but my soul is at peace."

"But, Brother," they queried, "if God wished you to suffer these pains for ten years, would you be resigned?"

"I would," he said, "not only for that number of years; but if God willed that I should endure my pains until Judgment Day, I would consent willingly; and I would still hope that He would give me the grace to be always content."

That is how great the patience of Brother Lawrence was at the beginning and during the course of his sickness, which lasted only four days.

But as the hour of his departure from this world approached, he redoubled his fervor. His faith became more lively, his hope firmer and his charity more ardent. The vigor of his faith can be judged by his frequent exclamations, showing the singular esteem he had for this virtue: "O faith, faith," he would say, expressing its excellence more by that than if he had said many things about it. Penetrated with its grandeur and enlightened by its radiance, he adored God ceaselessly and used to say that this adoration had occurred within him, as if naturally. He said one time to a religious that he hardly *believed* any longer in the dwelling of God in his soul; but that by means of this luminous faith he already *saw* something of this intimate presence.

The firmness of his hope was no less evident. So great was his fearlessness upon a journey where there is everything to fear, that he said to one of his friends who was questioning him upon it that he feared neither death, nor hell, nor the judgment of God, nor all the efforts of the devil. Indeed, he remarked that he saw the latter going and coming around his bed, but that he was mocking him. As people enjoyed hearing him say such edifying things, they continued to question him. They asked him whether he knew that it is a terrible thing to fall into the hands of the living God, because no one knows for certain whether he deserves love or hatred. "I admit it," he said; "but I would not want to know, for fear of being vain." He carried his abandonment to such lengths that, forgetting himself and considering only God and the accomplishment of His will, he said: "Yes, if by impossibility one could love God in hell and He willed to put me there, I would not care; for He would be with me and His presence would make it Paradise. I have abandoned myself to Him; He will do with me whatever He pleases."

If he loved God so much during his life, he did not love Him less at death. He was continually making acts of love. A religious having asked him whether he loved God with his whole heart, he answered, "Oh, if I knew that my heart did not love God, I would tear it out right now."

Since his sickness was visibly growing worse, they administered to him all the Last Sacraments, which he received joyously, with full knowledge and sane mind, which lasted until his final sigh.

Although they did not leave him alone a minute day or night and gave him all the aid which he would expect of the charity of his Brothers, still they did let him repose a little to profit by the last moments of life, which are so precious, and to reflect upon the great grace that God had just granted him, of receiving all the sacraments. Brother Lawrence employed this time very usefully in asking of God the final perseverance of his holy love. A religious having asked him what he was doing and with what his spirit was occupied, he replied: "I am doing what I will do for all eternity. I am blessing God, praising God, adoring Him and loving Him with all my heart. That is our whole profession, Brothers, to adore God and to love Him, without worrying about the rest." When a religious recommended himself to his prayers and begged him to obtain for him from God the true spirit of prayer, he told him that he must coöperate and endeavor on his side to render himself worthy of it; those were the last sentiments of his heart. The next day, which was Monday, the twelfth of February, 1691, about nine o'clock in the morning, without having any agony, without losing the use of his senses, without any convulsion,

Brother Lawrence of the Resurrection died in the embrace of the Lord and gave back his soul to God with the peace and tranquillity of a person falling asleep. His death was, indeed, like a gentle slumber which helped him pass from this unhappy life to a blessed one. For if one may judge what follows death by the holy actions that have preceded it, what thoughts may one not have of Brother Lawrence, who went from this world laden with good deeds and merits! It is easy to conclude —and one may presume it without flattery—that his death was precious in the sight of the Lord, that it was very quickly followed by his reward, that his lot is among the saints and that even now he is enjoying glory; that his faith is rewarded by clear vision, his hopes by possession, and his budding charity by a consummate love.

The Ways of Brother Lawrence

BY M. L'ABBÉ JOSEPH DE BEAUFORT

I AM WRITING what I myself have heard and seen of the ways of Brother Lawrence, Discalced Carmelite, who died in the Paris monastery about twelve years ago, and whose memory is in benediction. Although a eulogy and some letters of this good Brother have already been given to the public, I think we cannot too often review the memories of him that have been preserved.

Brother Lawrence himself shall speak to you. I will give you his very words in the interviews I had with him, which I wrote down as soon as I had left him. No one depicts the saints better than themselves. The confessions and the letters of Saint Augustine make a portrait of him far more natural than everything else that could be said of him; just so, nothing will make for a better understanding of the servant of God whose virtues I want to describe to you than what he himself said in the simplicity of his heart.

The goodness of Brother Lawrence did not render him at all severe. He had a genial presence, which gave confidence and made one feel immediately that one could reveal anything to him and that one had found a friend. On his part, when he knew those with whom he had to deal, he spoke freely and showed extreme kindness. What he used to say was simple, but always right and full of meaning. Beneath a common exterior could be perceived a singular wisdom, an assurance above the ordinary reach of a poor lay brother, a penetration far surpassing all that might have been expected of him.

He himself has depicted his dispositions and his interior conduct in the interviews that I am giving you. His conversion began, as you will there observe, with a profound conception of the power and the wisdom of God, which he carefully cultivated by a great fidelity in dismissing every other thought.

As this first knowledge of God was afterwards the seed of all the perfection of Brother Lawrence, it is opportune to dwell upon it a little while, in order to consider his conduct in this regard. Faith was the only light he used—not only to know God in the beginning, but never afterward did he wish to employ anything but faith to teach himself and guide him in all the ways of God. He told me many times that everything he heard others say, everything he found in books, all that he himself wrote seemed to him pale in comparison with what faith disclosed to him of the grandeur of God and of Jesus Christ.

"He alone," he used to say, "is capable of making Himself known as He really is; we search in reasoning and in the sciences, as in a poor copy, for what we neglect to see in an excellent original. God Himself paints Himself in the depths of our soul, and we do not wish to see Him there; we quit Him for chatter and disdain to converse with our King, Who is always present within us. It is too little," Brother Lawrence continued, "to love God and to know Him by what books tell us about Him, or by what we feel in our souls through some little impressions of devotion or some inspiration. We must enliven our faith and elevate ourselves by means of it above all our feelings, to adore God and Jesus Christ in all Their divine perfections, such as They are in Themselves. This way of faith is the mind of the Church and it suffices to arrive at high perfection."

Not only did he contemplate God present in his soul by faith; but in all that he saw, in all that happened, he raised his heart at once, passing from the creature to the Creator. A tree that he noticed to be barren in winter made him immediately think of God and inspired in him so sublime a realization that forty years afterwards it was still as strong and vivid in his soul as when he had received it. In this manner he was accustomed to act on all occasions, using visible things only to arrive at those invisible.

For the same reason, in the little reading that he did, he preferred the holy Gospel to all other books, because in it he found the wherewithal to nourish his faith most simply and most purely in the very words of Jesus Christ.

It was by fidelity in cultivating in his heart this deep *presence of God,* considered by faith, that Brother Lawrence began. He occupied himself with continual acts of adoration, love, invocation of the help of Our Lord in what he had to do. He thanked Him after having done it, he asked His pardon for his negligence, while confessing it, as he said, without making excuses to God. As these acts were so united to his occupations and the latter furnished him matter for them, he made them with the more ease. Thus, far from distracting him from his work, they helped him to do it well.

He admits, however, that he had had some difficulty about it at first, that he did pass some time without remembering his exercise; but that, after having humbly confessed his fault, he took up the practice again without trouble.

Sometimes a crowd of extravagant thoughts violently took the place of God and he contented himself with setting them aside gently, to return to his customary converse. Finally, his fidelity merited the recompense of a continual remembrance of God. His different and multiple acts were changed into a simple regard, into an enlightened love and an enjoyment without interruption.

> "The time of action," he said, "does not differ at all from that of prayer; I possess God as tranquilly in the bustle of my kitchen—where sometimes several people are asking me different things at one time—as if I were on my knees before the Blessed Sacrament. My faith sometimes even becomes so enlightened that I think I have lost it; it seems to me that the curtain of obscurity is drawn, that the endless, cloudless day of the other life is beginning to dawn."

This is the height to which our good Brother had been led by the fidelity he had displayed in rejecting every other thought in order to occupy himself with continual converse with God. At last it had become such a habit with him that he said it was practically impossible to turn away from it, to busy himself with anything else.

You will find in his conversations an important remark upon this subject, when he says that this presence of God has to be maintained rather by the heart and by love than by understanding and speech.

"In the way of God," he says, "thoughts count for little, love does everything.

"And it is not necessary," he continues, "to have great things to do." (I am depicting for you a lay brother in the kitchen, so please allow me to use his own phrases.) "I turn my little omelette in the pan for the love of God; when it is finished, if I have nothing to do, I prostrate myself on the ground and adore my God, Who gave me the grace to make it, after which I arise, more content than a king. When I cannot do anything else, it is enough for me to have lifted a straw from the earth for the love of God.

"People seek for methods of learning to love God," he continues. "They hope to arrive at it by I know not how many different practices; they take much trouble to remain in the presence of God in a quantity of ways. Is it not much shorter and more direct to do everything for the love of God, to make use of all the labors of one's state in life to show Him that, and to maintain His presence within us by this communion of our hearts with His? There is no finesse about it, one has only to do it generously and simply."

I piously preserve his own words.

One must not, nevertheless, suppose that to love God it is sufficient to offer Him his works, to invoke His aid and to produce acts of love of Him. Through these means our Brother arrived at the perfection of love only because from the beginning he had been very careful to do nothing which could displease God; because he had renounced everything else but Him and had entirely forgotten himself.

"Since my entrance into religion," such are his words, "I have no longer thought of virtue nor of my salvation. After having given myself wholly to God in satisfaction for my sins, and having renounced for His sake everything that is not He, I have trusted that I had nothing else to do for the rest of my days than to live as if there were no one but God and me in the world."

Thus Brother Lawrence began in the most perfect way, in leaving all for God and doing everything for love of Him. He had entirely forgotten himself. He no longer thought of heaven nor hell, nor of his past sins nor of those he was committing, after he had asked pardon of God for them. He never went back over his confessions; he entered into perfect peace when he had confessed his faults to God and knew nothing else to do. After that he abandoned himself to God, as he said, for life and death, for time and eternity.

"We are made for God alone," he used to say. "He would never disapprove our abandoning ourselves in order to think of Him. In Him we shall see what we need better than we would perceive it in ourselves by all our meditations; and it cannot be anything else than a remnant of self-love which, under pretence of our perfection, attaches us still to ourselves and hinders us from raising our hearts to God."

The Brother said that in the great anguish that he had suffered for four years—so great that all the men in the world could never have taken out of his mind the thought that he would be damned —he had not changed one whit his first determination; but that, without reflecting upon what would become of him and without considering his worry (as all distressed souls do), he had consoled himself by saying: "No matter what happens, at least I will do all my actions for the rest of my life for the love of God." By thus forgetting himself, he had indeed been willing to lose himself for God, in Whom he had actually found himself.

In him, the love of the will of God had taken the place of the attachment one usually has to his own will. In everything that happened to him he saw nothing but the plan of God, which kept him in continual peace. When people told him of some great abuse, far from being astonished at it he was surprised, on the contrary, that it was not still greater, considering the malice of which the sinner was capable. At once raising his heart to God and seeing that He could remedy it and that nevertheless He permitted these evils for reasons very just and very useful to the general order of His rule over the world, he prayed for the sinners. Then he did not distress himself any more about it and remained in peace.

One day I told him, without any preparation, that something of great consequence, which he had much at heart, and upon which he had been working for a long time, could not be done; that a resolution against it had just been made. To this he gave me no answer but, "We must believe that those who made the decision have good reasons. We have only to carry it out and say no more about it." This he did, and so completely that, although he has often since had occasion to speak of it, he has never opened his mouth on the subject.

A man of great worth, having visited Brother Lawrence in a serious illness, asked him what he would choose if God offered either to leave him alive a while in order to increase his merits, or to receive him into Heaven at once. Without any deliberation the good Brother answered that he would leave the choice to God and that for himself he had nothing else to do but wait until God showed him His will.

This disposition left him in such great indifference to everything and such entire liberty that it approached that of the blessed. He belonged to no party. There was evident in him no tendency nor inclination.

The natural attachment to one's country that people carry with them into even the holiest places did not preoccupy him. He was equally loved by those who had opposite inclinations. He wished for good in general, without regard to the people by whom, or for whom, it was done. Citizen of heaven, he was concerned with nothing on earth; his views were not limited by time; since for a long period he had contemplated nothing but the Eternal One, he had become eternal like Him.

Everything was the same to him—every place, every employment. The good Brother found God everywhere, as much while he was repairing shoes as while he was praying with the community. He was in no hurry to make his retreats, because he found in his ordinary work the same God to love and adore as in the depth of the desert.

His only means of going to God being to do everything for love of Him, he was indifferent as to being occupied with one thing or another, provided that he did it for God. It was He, and not the thing, that Brother considered. He knew that, the more the thing he did was opposed to his natural inclination, the greater was the merit of his love in offering it to God; that the pettiness of the deed would not diminish the worth of his offering, because God, needing nothing, considers in our works only the love that accompanies them.

Another characteristic of Brother Lawrence was an extraordinary firmness, which in another walk of life would have been called fearlessness, that showed a magnanimous soul, elevated above the fear and the hope of all that was not God. He admired nothing; nothing astonished him; he feared nothing. This stability of his soul came from the same source as all his other virtues. The exalted concept of God that he had made him think of Him, as He is indeed, as sovereign Justice and infinite Goodness. Trusting in this thought, he was confident that God would not deceive him and that He would do him only good, since he, on his part, was resolved never to displease Him, to do and suffer all for love of Him.

I asked him one day who was his director. He told me that he had none and that he did not think he needed one, since the rule and the duties that he had in religion pointed out to him what he had to do exteriorly, and the Gospel obliged him to love God with all his heart. Knowing this, he felt that a director would be useless to him; but he had great need of a confessor to remit his sins.

Those who conduct themselves in the spiritual life only according to their dispositions and special feelings, who think they have nothing more important to do than to examine whether they have devotion or not, could never have stability or a certain rule of life; because these dispositions change continually, either through our own negligence or through the designs of God, Who varies His gifts and His conduct towards us according to our needs.

The good Brother, on the contrary, firm in the way of faith, which never changes, was always the same, because he tried only to fulfill the duties of the post in which God set him, counting for merit only upon the virtues of his state. Instead of paying attention to his dispositions and examining the route by which he was going, he looked only at God, the end of his journey, moving towards Him at a great pace by the practice of justice, charity and humility, busier about doing than about considering what he was doing.

The devotion of Brother Lawrence, built upon this solid foundation, was not dependent upon visions or other extraordinary occurrences. He was persuaded that even those which are genuine are most often the marks of the weakness of a soul that depends more upon the gifts of God than upon God himself. Apart from the time of his novitiate, there were none of these sorts of things in his life; at least, he said nothing about them to the people in whom he had most confidence and to whom he opened his heart. All his life he walked in the footsteps of the saints, by the sure way of faith. He never departed from the ordinary road that leads to salvation by the exercises always authorized in the Church, by the practice of good works and of the virtues of his state; to him, all the rest was suspect. His great common sense and the light he had from the simplicity of his faith protected him against all the reefs that are met in the course of the spirit, upon which so many souls are shipwrecked today because they give themselves over to love of novelty, to their own imagination, to curiosity and to human advice.

Prepared by such a life and following so safe a course, he was not disturbed at the approach of death. During his whole life his patience had been great; but it increased when he approached his end. He never seemed to have a moment of sorrow, even in the greatest violence of his illness. Joy appeared not only on his countenance, but even in his manner of speaking; which constrained some religious, who used to go to visit him, to ask whether actually he were not suffering. "Excuse me," he said. "I am in pain. The pleurisy in my side hurts; but my soul is at peace." "But," they added, "if God wanted you to suffer these pains for ten years, would you be content?" "I would," he said, "not only for that number of years; but if God wanted me to endure my sickness until the day of judgment, I would willingly consent. I would even hope that He would give me the grace to be always resigned."

When the hour of his departure from this world was approaching, he cried out repeatedly, "Oh, faith, faith!" expressing its excellence better by that than if he had said more about it. He adored God continually and said to a religious that he scarcely believed any longer in the dwelling of God within his soul, but that by means of this luminous faith, he already saw something of this intimate presence.

So great was his fearlessness in a journey where there is everything to fear, that he said to one of his friends who was questioning him on this point that he feared neither death, nor hell, nor the judgment of God, nor the efforts of the devil.

As they liked to hear him say such edifying things, they continued to ply him with questions. They asked him whether he knew that it is a terrible thing to fall into the hands of the living God, because no one whatsoever is sure whether he is worthy of love or hatred. "I admit it," he said;

"but I would not want to know, for I would be afraid of becoming vain. Nothing is better than to abandon oneself to God."

After he had received the Last Sacraments, a religious asked him what he was doing, and with what his soul was occupied. "I am doing," he replied, "what I will do for all eternity. I am blessing God, praising Him, adoring Him and loving Him with all my heart. That is our profession, Brothers, to adore God and to love Him, without bothering about the rest."

These were the last sentiments of Brother Lawrence, who died a little while afterwards with the peace and tranquillity with which he had lived. His death occurred on the twelfth of February, 1691, when he was about eighty years old.

Nothing presents a better portrait of a true Christian philosopher than what has just been related of the life and the death of this good religious. Such were the men of former days who used to renounce the world, really not to occupy themselves any longer with anything but cultivating their souls and knowing God and His Son Jesus Christ— religious men who had for their rule the Gospel, and who professed the holy philosophy of the Cross. It is in this way that Saint Clement of Alexandria describes them to us, and he seems to have had in view a man like Brother Lawrence when he said that the great occupation of the philosopher, that is to say of the Christian sage, is prayer. He prays everywhere—not using many words, but in secret in the depths of his soul, whether out walking, or in repose, during reading or work. He praises God continually; not only upon rising in the morning and at noon, but in all his actions he renders glory to God, as did those seraphs of Isaias. The application to spiritual things that he has through prayer makes him gentle, affable, patient, and at the same time severe to the point of not even being tempted; he gives no hold upon himself either to pleasure or to sorrow. The joy of contemplation, upon which he feeds continually without ever being satiated, does not permit him to feel the little pleasures of earth. Through love he dwells with the Lord, although his body still appears on the earth; and after having shared, through faith, in the inaccessible light, he has no more relish for the goods of this world. By charity he is already where he ought to be and desires nothing, because he has the object of his desire, as far as it is possible.

He has no need of daring, because nothing in this life is troublesome to him nor capable of turning him away from the love of God. He has no need of calming himself, because he does not fall into sadness, persuaded as he is that all is going well. He does not become angry, nothing disturbs him, because he is always loving God and wholly absorbed in Him alone. He is not jealous, because he does not need anything. He does not love anyone with ordinary friendship, but he loves the Creator through creatures. His soul is set in constancy, exempt from all change, while, forgetting all the rest, he is attached solely to God.

Although Brother Lawrence passed his life in retirement, still there is nobody in any state of life who cannot draw great profit from what is here related of his conduct. He will teach persons engaged in the world to address themselves to God to ask His grace for doing their duty, even while they are performing their business, or in conversation, or in the midst of their recreations. By his example, they will be moved to thank God for His benefits, for the good that He helps them to do, and to humble themselves before Him because of their faults.

This is not a theoretical devotion, nor one that can be practised only in cloisters. Everyone is obliged to adore and to love God; and no one can perform these two great duties as he ought without establishing with God an interchange of love that makes us have recourse to Him at every moment, like children who can scarcely stand without their mother's help.

Not only is this far from difficult, but it is easy and necessary for everyone; it is that continual prayer that Saint Paul exacts of all Christians. Whoever does not do it does not feel his needs, nor his incapacity for any good; he does not know what he is, nor what God is, nor the continual need he has of Jesus Christ.

The business and intercourse of the world cannot serve as an excuse for neglecting one's duty. God is everywhere: in every place one can address Him, can make one's heart speak to Him in a thousand ways. With just a little love, one would not find it hard.

Persons retired from the bustle of the world have still more advantage to be gained from the example of Brother Lawrence. As they are delivered from most of the necessities and conventions of the world, which fill those that are involved in them with many cares, nothing can hinder them from renouncing, as this good Brother did, every other thought than that of doing all their actions for the love of God—from giving Him, as he said, everything for everything.

The example of his general detachment, of the entire forgetfulness of himself which he carried so far as to think no longer of his own salvation in order to occupy himself solely with God, his indifference to all sorts of employment or occupation, his freedom of spirit in matters of devotion, could not but be very useful to them.

Interviews

August 3, 1666.

I saw Brother Lawrence for the first time. He told me that God had given him a singular grace in his conversion, when he was still in the world and eighteen years old. He said that, one winter day as he was looking at a tree stripped of its leaves and considering that some time later these leaves would appear again, then flowers, then fruits, he received a profound impression of the providence and the power of God, which was never effaced from his soul. He declared that this impression detached him entirely from the world and gave him such a love of God that he could not say whether it had ever increased in the more than forty years since he had received this grace.

He said he had been a lackey of M. de Fuibert, the treasurer of the *Epargne*, and had been a clumsy lout who used to break everything.

He declared that he had asked to enter religion, believing that they would flay him for the clumsiness and the faults he would commit and that thereby he would sacrifice to God his life and all his fun; but that God had deceived him, for in it he had found nothing but satisfaction. This had often made him say to God: "Thou hast deceived me."

Brother insisted that one must form a habit of thinking of the presence of God by conversing with Him continually, and that it was a shameful thing to abandon conversation with Him in order to consider trifles.

One must nourish one's soul with an exalted conception of God, and thence we will derive a great joy at being His.

He said we must enliven our faith; that it was a pitiful thing that we should have so little faith; and that, instead of taking it for our rule and guide, we amused ourselves with petty devotions that changed every day. This road of faith was the spirit of the Church and it sufficed to lead to high perfection.

He remarked that one must give oneself entirely to God in pure abandonment, for temporal and spiritual affairs, and seek one's happiness in the doing of His will, whether He should lead us by suffering or by consolation. It should be all the same to one who was truly abandoned.

He said we would need fidelity, in the dryness by which God would test our love for Him.

It was in this state that we would make good acts of resignation and of abandonment, one of which alone often advanced us much on our way.

In the unhappiness and sins that he heard mentioned every day, Brother said, instead of being astonished at them, he was on the contrary surprised that they were not still more numerous, considering the malice of which the sinner is capable. He said that he prayed for him, but knowing that God could remedy the matter when He willed, he did not worry any more about it.

In order to succeed in abandoning ourselves to God as much as He desired of us, we must watch carefully over all the movements of the soul, which are involved in spiritual matters as well as in the most common things. God gave light for this to people who had a genuine desire to be His. If I had this intention, I could visit him whenever I liked, without fear of boring him; without it, I must not come to see him.

SECOND CONVERSATION

September 28, 1666.

Brother Lawrence said he had always governed himself by love, without any other interest, without bothering whether he would be damned or saved.

Still, having made it the intention of all his actions that he would do them all for the love of God, he had found himself quite well off. He was content when he could pick up a straw from the ground for the love of God, since he sought Him alone and not His gifts.

He declared that this disposition of his soul obliged God to give him infinite graces, but that in taking the fruit of these graces—that is to say, the love born of them—one must put aside the savor of it, saying that all that was not God, because one knew by faith that He was infinitely greater and quite otherwise than what one felt about Him. In this manner of acting, a wondrous contest occurred between God and the soul: God giving and the soul denying that what she received was God. In this contest the soul was as strong and stronger than God, because He could never give so much but that she could always deny that He was what He was giving.

He said that ecstasy and rapture belonged only to a soul that amused itself with the gift instead of rejecting it and going beyond the gift to God. Apart from surprise, one should not let oneself be carried away in this manner; however, God was the Master.

So magnificently and so promptly did God reward all that was done for Him, that he had sometimes wished he could hide from God what he was doing for love of Him; thus, not receiving the reward, he would have the pleasure of doing something solely for God.

He said he had suffered great tribulation of spirit, believing certainly that he was damned; that all the men in the world could not have taken this opinion from him, but that he had reasoned about it in this way: "I came into religion only for the love of God, I have tried to act only for Him. Whether I be damned or saved, I wish to continue to act purely for the love of God. I shall have at least this much good, that until death I will do what I can to love Him." This distress had lasted four years, during which he had suffered very much. Since then, he had thought neither of heaven nor of hell; all his life was simply freedom and continual rejoicing. He set his sins between God and himself, as if to tell Him that he did not deserve His graces, but that did not hinder God from overwhelming him with them. He took him sometimes by the hand and led him before the heavenly court, to show off the miserable one whom it pleased Him to honor.

In the beginning, Brother declared, a little effort was needed to form the habit of conversing continually with God and telling Him all that one was doing; but after a bit of care one would feel oneself awakened by His love, without any trouble.

He said that he expected that, after the good time that God was giving him, he would have his turn and his share in pains and sufferings; but that he did not worry about it, knowing well that, since he could do nothing by himself, God would not fail to give him the strength to bear them.

He remarked that he always applied to God when he was proposing to himself the practice of some virtue, saying to Him: "My God, I would not be able to do that, if Thou didst not help me," and that immediately he was given enough strength and more.

When he had sinned, he said, he did nothing else but admit his fault and say to God: "I will never do anything else, if Thou dost leave me to myself. Thou must hinder me from falling and correct whatever is not right." After that he did not worry about his sin.

Brother pointed out that one must act very simply with God and speak to Him frankly, asking

His help with things as they turn up; that God did not fail to give it, as he had often experienced.

He said that he had been told, a few days before, to go into Burgundy in order to get supplies of wine, and that this was very trying to him because, besides the fact that he had no head for business, he was lame in one leg and could not walk on the boat without rolling against the barrels. However, he did not worry about his awkwardness, any more than about his whole purchase of wine. He simply told God that it was His affair, after which he found that everything turned out nicely.

He had also been sent into Auvergne the previous year for the same purpose. He could not say how the business was done, he said; it was not he who did it, but it was very well done.

The same way, in the kitchen, for which he had the greatest natural aversion, having accustomed himself to do everything for the love of God and to ask His grace on every occasion to do his work, he had developed a very great facility during the fifteen years that he had been occupied there.

He said that at present he was in the shoe-repair shop that he liked very much, but that he was ready to leave this job like the others, merely rejoicing everywhere in being able to do little things for the love of God.

He declared that the time of prayer was not for him different from any other time; that he made his retreats when the Father Prior told him to, but that he did not desire them nor ask for them, since his greatest labor did not distract him from God.

Knowing that God should be loved in everything and laboring to fulfill this duty, he said that he did not need a director but a confessor, that he might receive absolution for his faults. He declared that he did indeed perceive his faults and was not surprised at them, that he confessed them to God and did not plead with Him to make excuses for them; but that afterwards he re-entered peacefully into his customary exercise of love and adoration.

In his distress, he stated, he had not consulted anyone; but with the light of faith, knowing only that God was present, he had contented himself with acting for Him, no matter what might happen, and that thus he had been willing to lose himself for the love of God, in Whom he had indeed found himself.

He remarked that thoughts spoiled everything; that the evil began there. He declared that we must be careful to reject thoughts as soon as we perceived that they were not things necessary to our present occupation or our salvation, so as to resume our conversation with God, in which we were at ease.

He had often passed the whole time of prayer, at the beginning of his conversion, in rejecting distractions and falling into them again.

Brother said that he had never been able to meditate according to a method, as the others did; that, however, in the beginning he had dwelt on thoughts for some time, but that afterwards he did not know how it went and it would be impossible for him to give an account of it.

He said he had asked to remain always a novice, thinking that they would not want to admit him to profession, and not being able to believe that his two years had passed.

He remarked that he was not bold enough to ask God for penances, that he did not even want to do any, but that he knew he deserved a great many of them; and when God sent him some, He would give him the grace to do them.

All penances and other exercises, he thought, served only to lead us to union with God through love. After having considered the matter well, he found it much shorter to go straight to the point by a continual practice of love, in doing everything for the love of God.

He said a sharp distinction should be drawn between acts of the understanding and those of the will—that the former were of small account and the latter, everything; that we have only to love and to rejoice in God.

Even if we should do all possible penances, he declared, if they were separated from love, they would not serve to wipe out a single sin. Without worrying, we should wait for remission of sins through the blood of Jesus Christ, laboring only to love Him with all our hearts. God seemed often to choose those who had been the greatest sinners to give them His greatest graces, rather than those who had remained in innocence, because that showed His goodness more.

Brother said that he was not thinking of death, nor of his sins, nor of heaven, nor of hell, but only of doing little things for the love of God, since he could not do big ones; after that, anything that God pleased could happen to him, for he was not anxious about it.

Although they should flay him alive, he declared, it would be nothing in comparison with an interior distress he had suffered, nor with the great joys that he had experienced and still had often. Therefore he did not worry about anything, nor fear anything, asking God for nothing except that he might not offend Him.

He told me that he had scarcely any scruples, for "when I realize that I have sinned I agree and say, 'That is my nature, the only thing I know how to do.' If I have not sinned, I thank God for it and confess that this grace comes from Him."

THIRD CONVERSATION

November 22, 1666

He told me that the foundation of his spiritual life had been an exalted concept and esteem of God in faith. Having once conceived this well, he had had no other care than to reject in the beginning every other thought, so as to do all his actions for the love of God. Having sometimes passed a long period without thinking of Him, he did not grow upset about it, but having confessed his weakness to God, he returned to Him with all the more confidence because he had found himself so unhappy as to forget Him so.

He said that the confidence we have in God honors Him very much and draws great graces upon us.

He declared that it was impossible, not only that God should deceive, but even that He should per-

mit to suffer for long a soul that is wholly abandoned to Him and resolved to endure everything
for Him.

Brother stated that he had attained to having
no thoughts except of God; and when he wished
to remove some other thought or temptation that
he had felt coming, the experience he had had of
the prompt assistance of God caused him sometimes
to let them advance—and when it was time, ad-
dressing himself to God, he found them vanish
right away.

Akin to this same experience, when he had some
exterior business he did not think about it in advance; but in the time necessary for the action, he
found in God as in a clear mirror what it was necessary that he do for the present. For some time he
had acted in this way, without any care before-
hand; but previous to this experience of the swift
help of God in his affairs, he did use to employ fore-
sight.

He said he had no memory of the things he did
and paid almost no attention even while he did
them—that upon rising from table, he did not
know what he had eaten. Acting in simplicity in
His sight, he did everything for the love of God,
thanking Him for having directed his actions, and
making an infinity of other acts; but all this very

calmly, in a way that held him attached to the loving presence of God.

When exterior occupations diverted him a little from the thought of God, there came to him from the Lord some remembrance which took possession of his soul, giving him some most engrossing idea of God. At times this set him so on fire that he cried out and felt violent impulses to sing and leap about like a crazy man.

Brother declared he was much more united to God in his ordinary occupations than when he left them to make the exercises of retreat, from which he usually issued with great dryness of spirit.

He said that he expected to have in the future some great pain of body or soul, and that his worst trial would be to lose the sensible presence of God, which he had had for so long a time; but that the goodness of God made him certain that He would not leave him entirely and that He would give him the strength to endure whatever evil He might permit to come to Him. With this assurance, he was not afraid of anything and had no need of discussing his soul with anyone. When he had attempted to do so, he had always ended by being more distressed. He added that, in wishing to die and lose himself for the love of God, he had no apprehension; that entire abandonment to God was the secure road in which one would always have enough light to guide one.

In the beginning one must be faithful, he said, both in acting and in renouncing self; but after that there were only ineffable delights. In difficulties one need only turn to Jesus Christ and pray for His grace, with which everything became easy.

He remarked that people stopped at penances and particular devotions, neglecting love, which is their purpose; that this could easily be seen in their actions, and was the reason of their possessing so little solid virtue.

Neither skill nor knowledge were needed, he declared, to go to God—only a heart resolved to think solely of Him and for Him, and to love no one but Him.

FOURTH CONVERSATION

November 25, 1667

Brother Lawrence spoke to me with great fervor and openness of his manner of going to God, about which I have already written.

He said to me that everything consisted in renouncing, once for all, whatever we recognize as not leading to God, in order to accustom ourselves to a continual conversation with Him, without any mystery or finesse. We have only to recognize God, intimately present within us; to address ourselves to Him at all times in order to ask His help, to know His will in doubtful cases, and to do well what we clearly see that He wants of us. We should offer these acts to Him before doing them and thank Him afterwards for having done them for His sake.

In this continual conversation, we would also be occupied in praising, adoring and loving God incessantly for His infinite goodness and perfections.

Brother declared that we ought in all confidence to ask God's grace, without paying any attention to our thoughts, but trusting in the infinite merits of Our Lord. He said that God did not fail to give us His grace at each action and that he himself was sensibly aware of this. He sinned only at times when he was distracted from the company of God or when he had forgotten to ask His help.

In doubts, he remarked, God never fails to give light when people have no other design than to please Him and act for love of Him.

He said that our sanctification depends not upon the changing of our work, but upon doing for God what we ordinarily do for ourselves. It was a pity, he thought, to see how many people were attached to certain works, which they did quite imperfectly for several human considerations, always taking the means for the end.

He found no more excellent means for going to God, he said, than the ordinary tasks that were prescribed to him by obedience, purifying them as much as he could from all human respect and doing them for the pure love of God.

It was a great mistake, Brother said, to believe that the time of prayer should be different from the other, for we are as much obligated to be united to God by action, at the time of action, as by prayer in its time.

He declared that his prayer was nothing else than the presence of God, his soul having fallen asleep in Him to everything else but love. Outside of this time he found scarcely any difference, keeping himself always near to God to praise Him and bless Him with all his power. He thus passed his life in continual joy, hoping however that God would give him something to suffer when he would be stronger.

We must, for good and all, trust in God and abandon ourselves to Him alone. He will not deceive us.

We should never, Brother remarked, grow weary of doing little things for the love of God, Who regards not the greatness of the work but its love. We

must not be surprised at failing often in the beginning, for in the end would come a habit that would
make us produce our actions without thinking
about it and with wonderful pleasure.

He said that in order to attach ourselves entirely
to the will of God, we have only to cultivate faith,
hope and charity; that all the rest was of no im-
portance and we need not dwell upon it, except as
one would upon a bridge that one was crossing
very quickly in order to go lose himself in the sole
end by confidence and love.

All things are possible to him who believes; still
more to him who hopes; still more to him who
loves; and most of all, to him who practices and
perseveres in these three virtues.

The end that we should propose to ourselves is
to be, even in this life, the most perfect adorers of
God that we can, as we hope to be for all eternity.

Brother added that when we undertake the spiritual life we ought fundamentally to consider who
we are. Then we will find ourselves deserving of
all contempt, unworthy of the name of Christian,
subject to all sorts of miseries and to an infinity of
accidents that upset us and make us unstable in our
health, in our moods, in our interior and exterior
dispositions—in short, persons whom God wills to

humble by numberless pains and labors, within as well as without us.

After that, should we be astonished if we encounter pains, temptations, opposition and contradiction from our neighbor? Ought we not, on the contrary, submit to them and bear them as long as God wills, since they are things advantageous to us?

A soul is all the more dependent on grace, the more it aspires to high perfection.

Spiritual Maxims

ALL THINGS are possible to him who believes; still more to him who hopes; still more to him who loves; and most of all, to him who practices these three virtues and perseveres in them. All of those who are baptized, believing as they should, have taken the first step on the way of perfection, and will be perfect as long as they persevere in the practice of the following maxims.

I. Always to regard God and His glory in what we are doing, saying and undertaking: let the end that we propose be to become the most perfect adorers of God in this life, as we hope to be through all eternity. We must make a firm resolution to surmount, with God's grace, all the difficulties met with in the spiritual life.

II. When we undertake the spiritual life, we ought fundamentally to consider who we are; and we will find ourselves deserving of all contempt, unworthy of the name of Christian, subject to all sorts of miseries and to an infinity of accidents which upset us and render us unstable in our health, in our moods, in our interior and exterior disposition—in short, people whom God wills to humble by a countless number of pains and labors, within us as well as without.

III. Unquestionably we must believe that it is good for us and agreeable to God to sacrifice ourselves for Him; that it is usual for His divine Providence to abandon us to all sorts of states, to suffer all kinds of pains, miseries and temptations for the love of God and as long as He pleases—since, without this submission of heart and mind to the will of God, devotion and perfection cannot exist.

IV. A soul is all the more dependent upon the grace of God, the more it aspires to high perfection, and the help of God is so much the more needed at each moment, because without it the soul can do nothing. The world, the flesh and the devil together wage such fierce and continual war upon her that without this actual help and this humble, necessary dependence they would drag her down in spite of herself; that seems hard to nature, but grace is pleased with the condition and reposes in it.

PRACTICES NECESSARY TO ACQUIRE THE SPIRITUAL LIFE

1. The most holy, common and necessary practice in the spiritual life is the presence of God; that is, habitually to take pleasure in His divine company, speaking humbly and conversing with Him

lovingly at all seasons, at every minute, without rule or measure—above all, in the time of temptations, sorrows, dryness, distaste, even of infidelities and sins.

2. One must try continually so that all his actions without distinction may be a sort of little conversation with God; however, not in a studied way, but just as they happen, with purity and simplicity of heart.

3. We must do all our actions with deliberation and care, without impetuosity or precipitation, for these show a disordered spirit. We must work gently, calmly and lovingly with God, and beg Him to accept our work; by this continual attention to God we will break the demon's head and make his weapons fall from his hands.

4. During our work and other actions, even during our reading and writing on spiritual topics, more—during our exterior devotions and vocal prayers—let us stop a few minutes, as often as we can, to adore God in the depths of our hearts, to enjoy Him, as it were, in passing and in secret. Since you are not unaware that God is present before you during your actions, that He is in the depth and center of your heart, why should you not cease your exterior occupations—at least, from time to time—and even your vocal prayers, to adore Him

interiorly, to praise, petition Him, to offer Him your heart, and to thank Him?

What can there be more pleasing to God than thus a thousand times a day to leave all creatures in order to retire and worship Him in one's interior— unless it be to destroy the self-love which can exist only among creatures, of whom we are insensibly freed by these interior returns to God?

In short, we cannot give God greater pledges of our loyalty than by renouncing and contemning creatures a thousand times, to enjoy one single moment with the Creator.

I do not intend by that to oblige you to leave external things forever; that cannot be done. Prudence, the mother of virtues, must serve you for a guide. Nevertheless, I declare that it is a common mistake of spiritual persons not to leave external things from time to time to adore God within themselves and to enjoy in peace some few moments of His divine presence. This digression has been long, but I thought the subject required all that explanation. Let us return to our practices.

5. All this adoration should be made by faith, believing that God really is in our hearts; that He must be adored, loved and served in spirit and in truth; that He sees all that passes and will pass within us and in all creatures; that He is inde-

pendent of all, the One upon Whom all creatures depend. Infinite in all sorts of perfections, He merits by His infinite excellence and His sovereign rule all that we are and all that exists in Heaven and on earth, of which He can dispose at His good pleasure during time and eternity. In justice we owe Him all our thoughts, words and actions. Let us see whether we do this.

6. We must carefully examine which are the virtues most necessary for us, those most difficult to acquire, the sins into which we most frequently fall, and the most usual and unavoidable occasions of our falls. In the time of struggle we should have recourse to God with entire confidence and remain firm in the presence of His divine Majesty. We ought to adore Him humbly, declare to Him our misery and weakness, lovingly beg the aid of His grace. By this means we shall find in Him all virtues, even though we do not possess one.

HOW TO ADORE GOD IN SPIRIT AND IN TRUTH

There are three things in this question to be answered.

First, to adore God in spirit and in truth means, to adore Him as we should: God is a spirit, then He must be adored in spirit and in truth. That is to say, we must worship Him with a humble, sincere adoration of spirit in the depth and center of our souls. Only God can see this adoration, which we must repeat so often that at last it becomes natural to us, as if God were one with our soul and our soul were one with God; practice will demonstrate this.

Secondly, to adore God in truth is to recognize Him for what He is, and ourselves for what we are. To adore God in truth is to recognize truly, actually and in our heart that God is what He is—that is to say, infinitely perfect, infinitely adorable, infinitely apart from evil, and so with all the divine attributes. What man is there, however little sense he may have, who would not exert all his strength to pay his respect and adoration to this great God?

Thirdly, to adore God in truth is to admit, moreover, that we are just the opposite, and that He is willing to make us like Him, if we wish it. Who would be so rash as to turn aside for even a moment from the respect, the love, the service and the continual adoration that we owe Him?

OF THE UNION OF THE SOUL WITH GOD

Three kinds of unions exist: the first habitual, the second virtual and the third actual.

Habitual union occurs when one is united to God only by grace.

Virtual union exists when, commencing an action

by which one unites oneself to God, a person remains united to Him by virtue of this action, as long as it lasts.

Actual union is the most perfect kind. Wholly spiritual as it is, it makes its movement felt, because the soul is not asleep as in the other unions, but powerfully excited. Its operation is livelier than that of fire and more luminous than a sun undarkened by a cloud. However, one can be mistaken in this sentiment. It is not a simple expression of the heart, like saying, "My God, I love Thee with all my heart," or other similar words; it is an ineffable state of the soul—gentle, peaceful, devout, respectful, humble, loving and very simple—that urges and presses it to love God, to adore Him, even to embrace Him with inexpressible tenderness such as only experience can make us imagine.

All those who strive for divine union must know that everything which can rejoice the will is to it agreeable and delicious, or so considered.

Everyone must admit that God is incomprehensible and that to unite oneself to Him, we must deprive our wills of all sorts of tastes and pleasures of mind and body, so that, being thus disengaged, they can love God in everything. For if the will can in some manner comprehend God, it can be only by love. There is a great difference between the tastes and sentiments of the will and the acts of the same will, since the tastes and sentiments of the will are in the soul as in their limit, while its act, which is properly love, terminates in God as its End.

OF THE PRESENCE OF GOD

The presence of God is an application of our soul to God, or a remembrance of God present, which can be made either by the imagination or by the intellect.

I know a person who for forty years has practiced an intellectual presence of God, to which he gives several other names. Sometimes he calls it a simple act, or a clear and distinct knowledge of God, sometimes a vague view or general and loving look at God, a remembrance of God. Other times he terms it attention to God, mute intercourse with God, confidence in God, the life and the peace of the soul. To sum it up, this person has told me that all these manners of the presence of God are but synonyms which signify one identical thing, which is now natural to him, as I will describe.

He says that by means of acts, frequently recalling to his mind the presence of God, he has formed such a habit that, as soon as he is free of his exterior occupations and even often when he is most engaged in them, the tip of his spirit, or the highest part of his soul, rises without any effort on his part and remains as suspended and fixed in God, above all things, as in its center and place of repose. Since in this repose he feels his soul almost always accompanied by faith, that suffices. That is what he calls the actual presence of God, which includes all the other kinds of presence and much more. Now he lives as if there were no one but God and he in the world, he converses everywhere with God, asks Him for what he needs, and rejoices with Him ceaselessly in a thousand ways.

Nevertheless, one should realize that this conversation with God occurs in the depth and center of the soul. It is there that the soul speaks to God heart to heart, and always in a great and profound peace that the soul enjoys in God. Everything that happens outside is to the soul only a blaze of straw that goes out while it is catching fire, and scarcely ever disturbs its interior peace.

To return to our presence of God, I declare that this gentle and loving gazing at God insensibly lights in the soul a divine fire which so enkindles it with the love of God that a person is obliged to do many exterior things to temper it.

People would be surprised if they knew what the soul says to God sometimes. He seems to be so well pleased with these conversations that He permits everything to the soul, provided that it always wills to dwell with Him in its depths. As if He feared that it might return to creatures, He takes care to give it all that it could desire, so that it often finds within itself a refreshment very savory and delicious to its taste, although it may never have desired or procured it in any manner, and without even having contributed anything but its consent.

The presence of God is, then, the life and nourishment of the soul, which can be acquired with the grace of God. Here are the means to do so.

MEANS OF ACQUIRING THE PRESENCE OF GOD

1. The first means is a great purity of life.

2. The second, a great fidelity to the practice of this presence and to the interior gazing upon God in faith. This must always be done gently, humbly and lovingly, without giving way to any trouble or anxiety.

3. You must take particular care that this interior glance, although it may last only a moment, precedes your exterior acts, that from time to time it accompanies them, and that you finish all of them with it. Since time and much effort are needed to acquire this practice, one should not be discouraged when one fails, because a habit can be

formed only with difficulty; but when once it is formed, everything will be done with pleasure.

Is it not proper that the heart, which is the first to live and dominates all the other parts of the body, should be the first and the last to love God, whether upon beginning or ending all our spiritual or bodily actions, and generally in all the deeds of our lives? It is in the heart that we must carefully produce this little interior glance, which must be done as I have already said, without trouble and without contriving to make it easier.

4. It will not be out of place for those who are beginning this practice to form interiorly some phrase, such as, "My God, I am all Thine"; "God of love, I love Thee with all my heart"; "Lord, do with me according to Thy will"; or some other words that love inspires at the time. But they must take care that their mind does not wander nor return to creatures, and they must hold it attached to God alone, so that, pressed and forced by the will, it may be obliged to dwell with God.

5. This presence of God, a little painful in the beginning, operates in the soul marvelous effects when it is faithfully practiced. It draws down in abundance the graces of the Lord and conducts the soul insensibly to that pure gazing, that loving sight of God present everywhere, which is the holi-

est, the firmest, the easiest and the most efficacious manner of prayer.

6. Notice, please, that to arrive at this state we take for granted the mortification of the senses. It is impossible that a soul which still takes some pleasure in creatures can wholly enjoy this divine presence; for to be with God, one must absolutely leave creatures.

THE USEFULNESS OF THE PRESENCE OF GOD

1. The first fruit that the soul receives from the practice of the presence of God is that its faith is livelier and more active in all the circumstances of life, particularly in times of need, since this practice easily obtains for us grace in our temptations and in the inevitable intercourse that we must have with creatures. The soul, accustomed by this exercise to the practice of faith, by a simple act of memory sees and feels God present; she invokes Him easily, efficaciously, and obtains what she needs. One might say that in this she possesses something approaching the state of the Blessed: the more she advances, the more lively her faith becomes, and finally it grows so penetrating that she might almost say, "I no longer believe, but I see and experience."

2. The practice of the presence of God strength-

ens us in hope. Our hope increases in proportion to our knowledge—in the measure that our faith penetrates by this holy exercise into the secrets of the Divinity, in the measure that it discovers in God a beauty infinitely surpassing not only that of bodies that we see upon earth, but even that of the most perfect souls and that of the angels —our hope increases and grows stronger, and the greatness of the good that it expects to enjoy and that in some degree it tastes, reassures and sustains it.

3. This practice inspires in the will a contempt for created things and sets it aglow with the fire of holy love; because the soul is always with God, Who is a consuming fire and reduces into powder whatever can be opposed to Him. The soul thus enkindled can no longer live except in the presence of its God, a presence which produces in the heart a holy ardor, a sacred urgency and a violent desire to see this God, Who is loved, known, served and adored by all creatures.

4. By the presence of God and by this interior gaze the soul familiarizes itself with God to such an extent that it passes almost its whole life in continual acts of love, adoration, contrition, confidence, thanksgiving, offering, petition, and all the most excellent virtues. Sometimes it even becomes

one single act that does not end, because the soul is always in the ceaseless exercise of this Divine presence.

I know that there are few persons who arrive at this degree, for it is a grace with which God favors only some chosen souls, since this simple regard is a gift of His generous hand. But I will say, for the consolation of those who wish to embrace this holy practice, that He gives it ordinarily to those who dispose themselves for it; and if He does not, one can at least, with the help of His ordinary graces, acquire by the practice of the presence of God a method and state of prayer which approaches very closely to this simple gazing upon Him.

Letters of Brother Lawrence of the Resurrection

Paris, June 1, 1682

Dear Reverend Mother,

I am using the occasion of———to inform you of the thoughts of one of our religious upon the admirable results and the continual help that he receives from the presence of God. Let us both profit by them.

You should know that his principal endeavor, for the more than forty years that he has been in religion, has been to stay always with God and to do nothing, to say nothing, to think nothing that can displease Him—without any other intention than that of His pure love and because He deserves infinitely more than that.

Just now he is so accustomed to this Divine presence that he receives from it continual help on all sorts of occasions. For about thirty years his soul has enjoyed interior delights so ceaseless and sometimes so great that, in order to moderate them and prevent them from appearing, he is constrained to commit exteriorly childish acts which savor more of folly than of devotion.

If sometimes he is a little too absent from this Divine presence, God immediately makes Himself felt in his soul to recall him, a thing which often happens to him when he is the most engaged in his exterior occupations. He responds with exact fidelity to these interior attractions, either by raising his heart to God, or by a gentle and loving look, or by some words that love prompts at these meetings; for example, "My God, I am all Thine. Lord, do with me as Thou wilt." Then it seems to him, as indeed he feels, that this God of love, contenting Himself with these few words, goes to sleep again and reposes in the depth and center of his soul. The experience of these things renders him so certain that God is always in this depth of his soul that he cannot doubt it, whatever he does or whatever happens to him.

Judge from that, Reverend Mother, what contentment and satisfaction he enjoys, feeling continually within him so great a treasure. He is no longer anxious to find it, he does not worry any more about looking for it, for he has discovered it and is free to take from it what he will.

He often complains of our blindness and cries out ceaselessly that we are to be pitied for being content with so little. God has infinite treasures to give us, he says, and a little sensible devotion that passes in a minute satisfies us. He declares that we are blind, because in this way we tie God's hands and dam up the abundance of His graces; but when He finds a soul penetrated with a lively faith, He pours upon it graces in abundance. It is a torrent, held back by force from its ordinary channel, which, having found an exit, gushes out exuberantly.

Yes, often we stop this torrent by the slight esteem we have for it. Let us not arrest it any longer, my dear Mother. Let us enter into our hearts, break this dike, give light to grace, make up for lost time. Perhaps we have not long to live and death is on our heels. Let us take care: we die only once.

Once again, let us enter into ourselves, for time presses and there is no reprieve; each must fend for himself. I believe you have taken such wise measures that you will not be surprised, and I praise you for it—for that is our business. However, we must always labor, since in the life of the spirit not to advance is to recoil; yet, those who have the wind of the Holy Ghost sail even while they are asleep. If the bark of our soul is still tossed by winds or storm, let us awaken the Lord Who is reposing there, and He will swiftly calm the sea.

I have taken the liberty, my dear Mother, to inform you of these thoughts, in order to juxtapose them to your own. They will serve to rekindle and to set them afire, if by some misfortune (which may God not permit, for it would be a great mischance) they were growing even a trifle cold. Let us then recall, you and I, our first fervor. Let us profit by the example and the sentiments of this religious, little known by the world, but well known by God and tenderly caressed by Him. I will ask this grace for you; do you beg it earnestly for me.

SECOND LETTER

Dear Reverend Mother,

Today I have received two books and a letter from Sister————, who is preparing for her Profession and asks the prayers of your holy community and of yourself in particular. She has observed that I have a very great and singular confidence in them, so do not disappoint her, but beg of God that she may make her sacrifice with the sole thought of His love and a firm resolution to be all His. I will send you one of these books which treat of the presence of God. It is a practice after my own heart, in which all spiritual life consists, and it seems to me that in practicing it as one should, one becomes religious in a short time.

I know that for this end the heart must be emptied of everything else, God wishing to be the only one to possess it; and as He cannot be the only one to do so without emptying it of everything that is not He, so neither can He act in it or do with it what He would like.

There is not in the world any manner of living sweeter nor more delightful than continual intercourse with God. Only those who practice and taste it can understand this. However, I do not advise you to practice it for this motive—it is not consolations that we seek in this exercise—but let us do it out of love and because God wills it.

If I were a preacher, I would preach nothing else than the practice of the presence of God; and if I were a director of souls, I would urge it upon everyone, so necessary and even easy do I believe it to be.

Ah, if we knew the need we have of the grace and the help of God, we would never lose Him from sight for a moment. Trust me. Make right now a holy and firm resolution never deliberately to depart from Him, and to live the rest of your days in this holy Presence, deprived for the love of Him, if He thinks it best, of all consolations of heaven and earth. Set your hand to the task. If you do it as you should, be assured that you will soon see the effects of it. I will help you with my prayers, poor though they are. I earnestly recommend myself to yours and to those of your holy community.

THIRD LETTER

Paris, November 3, 1685

Dear Reverend Mother,

I have received from Miss————the rosaries that you entrusted to her. I am amazed that you did not send me your opinion of the book that I sent you, which you must have received. Practice it energetically in your old age, for it is better late than never.

I cannot understand how religious persons can live content without the practice of the presence of God. As for me, I stay retired with Him in the depth and center of my soul as much as I can, and when I am thus with Him I fear nothing; but the least detour is a hell to me.

This exercise does not kill the body. Still, it is proper to deprive the latter from time to time, and even often, of many little consolations, although they are innocent and permissible; for God does not allow a soul that wishes to be entirely His to take its consolations elsewhere than with Him. That is more than reasonable.

I do not say that for this cause one must torment

oneself. No, God must be served with holy freedom. We should labor faithfully, without trouble or anxiety, gently and calmly recalling our spirit to God as many times as we find it distracted from Him.

It is necessary, however, to place all our confidence in God and to rid ourselves of all other cares —even of a quantity of special devotions, which, although they may be good, have been undertaken rashly—since, after all, these devotions are only means to an end. So, when by this exercise of the presence of God we are with Him Who is our end, it is useless for us to return to the means. But we can continue our intercourse of love with Him, remaining in His holy presence: sometimes by an act of adoration, of praise, of desire; sometimes by an act of offering, of thanksgiving, and in all the ways that our spirit can invent.

Do not be discouraged by the repugnance that you may feel on the part of nature, for you must do violence to yourself. Often in the beginning we think the time is wasted, but we must continue and resolve to persevere in it until death and in spite of all difficulties. I recommend myself to the prayers of the holy community and to your own.

FOURTH LETTER

Dear Madam:

I pity you very much. If you can leave the care of your affairs to Mr. and Mrs.——— and not occupy yourself any longer with anything but prayer, you will do a wonderful thing. God does not ask much of us: a little remembrance from time to time, a little adoration, sometimes to ask His grace, sometimes to offer Him your pain, other times to thank Him for the graces He has given you and still gives, in the midst of your occupations to console yourself with Him as often as you can. During your meals and your conversations, sometimes raise your heart to Him, for the least little remembrance will always be very pleasing to Him. For this purpose you need not pray very loudly; He is nearer to us than we think.

In order to be always with God, it is not necessary to stay forever in the church; we can make our heart an oratory, into which we retire from time to time to converse with Him gently, humbly and lovingly. Everyone is capable of these familiar conversations with God—some more, others less; He knows what we can do. Let us begin. Perhaps He is only waiting for a generous resolution on our part. Courage, for we have but a short time to live: you are almost sixty-four years old and I am nearly eighty. Let us live and die with God. Pains will always be sweet and agreeable to us when we are with Him, and without Him the great pleasures will be to us a cruel torment. May He be blessed in everything! Amen.

Accustom yourself then, little by little, to adore Him in this way, to beg for His grace, to offer Him your heart from time to time—during the day, in the midst of your work, at every moment, if you can. Do not constrain yourself by rules or special devotions; do it in faith, with love and humility. You may assure Mr. and Mrs.———— and Miss————of my poor prayers, and that I am their servant, and particularly yours, in the Lord.

FIFTH LETTER

Dear Reverend Father:

Not finding my way of life in the books, although I am not at all worried about it, still for greater assurance I would like very much to know your opinion on the state in which I find myself.

A few days ago, in a private discussion with a person of devotion, she told me that the spiritual life is a life of grace, which begins with servile fear, grows through the hope of eternal life and is consummated by pure love; also, that different people have different degrees of achieving at last this blessed consummation.

I have not followed all these methods. On the contrary. I do not know why, but they scared me at first; this was the reason that, at my entrance into religion, I resolved to give myself entirely to God in satisfaction for my sins, and for love of Him to renounce all that was not He.

During the first years, I used to occupy myself in my ordinary prayers with thoughts of death, judgment, hell, heaven, and my sins. I continued in this way for several years, busying myself carefully for the rest of the day and even during my work with the presence of God, Whom I considered to be always near me, often even in the depth of my heart. This gave me so high an esteem for God that faith alone was capable of satisfying me on this point.

Insensibly I did the same thing during my prayers, which caused me great sweetness and consolation. This is how I began. I shall tell you, however, that during the first ten years I suffered very much; the fear that I had of not belonging to God as I would have wished, my past sins always present before my eyes, and the great graces that God gave me, were the matter and the source of all my ills. During this whole time I used to fall often, and to get up immediately. It seemed to me that creatures, reason, and even God were against me and that faith alone was on my side. I was sometimes troubled with the thought that this was an effect of my presumption in aspiring to be all of a sudden at a point which others reach only with difficulty; at other times, that I was wilfully destroying myself, that there was no salvation for me.

When I was not expecting anything more than to end my days in this trouble and anxiety (which did not at all lessen my confidence in God and served only to increase my faith) suddenly I found myself wholly changed. My soul, which until then was always troubled, felt a profound interior peace, as if it were in its center and a place of repose.

Since that time, I have been working before God simply, in faith, with humility and love; and I try carefully to do nothing, say nothing and think nothing that could displease Him. I hope that, when I have done what I can, He will do with me as He pleases.

As to telling you what is going on within me now, I cannot express it. I feel no anxiety nor doubt about my state, as I have no other wish than what God wants. I try in all things to do His will, and I am so submissive to it that I would not wish to lift a straw from the ground against His order, nor for any other motive than the pure love of Him.

I have given up all my private devotions and prayers which are not of obligation, and occupy myself only with holding myself ever in His holy presence. This I do by a simple attention and a general, loving gaze upon God, which I might call actual presence of God, or, better, a mute and secret intercourse of the soul with God, which scarcely ceases. I experience such contentment and joy, interior and even exterior, that in order to moderate it and prevent its becoming apparent, I am forced to do childish things that savor more of folly than devotion.

To sum up, Reverend Father, I cannot doubt that my soul has been with God for more than thirty years. I will pass over many things for fear of tiring you, but I believe I should indicate to you in what manner I consider myself before God, Whom I envisage as my King.

I regard myself as the most miserable of men, torn with wounds, filled with stenches, who has committed all sorts of crimes against his King; feeling a sensible remorse, I confess to Him all my evil deeds, I beg His pardon for them, I abandon myself into His hands, to do with me what He pleases. This King, full of goodness and mercy, far from chastising me, embraces me lovingly, makes me eat at His table, serves me with His own hands, gives me the keys of His treasury, and treats me in every way as His favorite. He converses with me and enjoys my company ceaselessly in a thousand manners, without speaking of pardoning me, nor taking away my former habits. Although I beg Him to do with me as He wills, I find myself always weaker and more miserable, but more caressed by God. That is how I look upon myself from time to time in His holy presence.

My most ordinary state is this simple attention, and this general, loving gaze upon God, to which I often find myself attached by sweetness and satisfaction greater than that which a baby feels at the breast of his nurse. If I dared to use the expression, I would willingly call this state "the breast of God," because of the inexpressible sweetness that I taste and experience in it.

If sometimes, through necessity or weakness, I turn away, I am immediately recalled by interior sentiments so charming and delightful that I am embarrassed to mention them. I beg you, Reverend Father, to reflect rather upon my great miseries, which you know well, than upon these great graces with which God favors my soul, unworthy and ungrateful though I am.

As to my hours of prayer, they are no more than a continuation of this same exercise. Sometimes, during them, I consider myself a piece of stone before a sculptor who intends to make a statue out of it. Presenting myself thus before God, I beg Him to form in my soul His perfect image and to render me wholly like to Him.

At other times, as soon as I recollect myself, I feel my whole mind and heart rise without care or effort and remain suspended, fixed in God as if in its center and place of repose.

I know that some people consider this state as laziness, deception and self-love. I declare that it is a holy laziness and a blessed self-love, if the soul in that state were capable of them; but, indeed, when it is in this repose, it cannot be disturbed by the acts it used to make, which were then its support, but now would only harm rather than help it.

However, I cannot permit anyone to call it deception, since the soul that in this state is enjoying God, does not desire anything but Him. If this is deception in me, then He must remedy it. Let Him do with me what He pleases, for I wish nothing but Him and to be all His. Still, you will do me a great favor to send me your opinion, to which I always defer, because I have a particular esteem for your Reverence.

SIXTH LETTER

Dear Reverend Mother:

Though my prayers have but little worth, they shall not fail you; I promised them to you, and I will keep my promise. How happy we would be, if we could find the treasure of which the Gospel speaks! All the rest would seem to us as nothing. As it is infinite, the more one explores it, the more riches does he find. Let us busy ourselves ceaselessly in looking for it and not grow weary until we have found it. . . .

*   *   *

Indeed, Reverend Mother, I do not know what will become of me. It seems that peace of soul and repose of spirit come to me while I am asleep. If I were capable of pain, it would be because I have none; and if I were permitted I would willingly console myself with the thought that there is a purgatory, in which I hope to suffer for the expiation of my sins. I do not know what God has in store for me; I am in such great tranquillity that I fear nothing. What could I fear, when I am with Him? I stay there as much as I can. May He be blessed for everything! Amen.

SEVENTH LETTER

October 12, 1688

Dear Madame,

We have a God infinitely good, Who knows what He is doing. I have always believed that He would reduce you to extremity. He will come in His good time, and when you least expect it. Hope in Him more than ever; thank Him with me for the graces He is giving you, particularly for the strength and patience He gives you in your afflictions, for it is an evident mark of His concern about you. Console yourself, then, with Him and thank Him for everything.

I admire also the strength and the courage of Mr.———. God has given him a fine nature and a good will, but he is still a little worldly and very young. I hope that the affliction which God has sent him will serve for a salutary medicine and make him enter into himself. This is an occasion to inspire him to place all his confidence in the One Who accompanies him everywhere. Let him remember Him as often as he can, especially in the greatest dangers.

A little lifting up of the heart suffices. A brief remembrance of God, an interior act of adoration, even while one may be running with sword in hand, are prayers which, however short they are, are nevertheless very pleasing to God. Far from destroying courage in those who are engaged in arms, even on the most dangerous occasions, they fortify them. Let him then remember God as much as he can and accustom himself little by little to this slight, but holy, exercise. No one sees it at all; there is nothing easier than to repeat often during the day these little interior acts of adoration. Recommend to him, if you please, that he should remember God as often as he can, in the way that I indicate to him here; it is very proper and necessary for a soldier, who is daily exposed to the danger of his life, and often of his salvation. I hope that God will assist him and all the family, whom I salute.

EIGHTH LETTER

Dear Reverend Mother,

You are not telling me anything new, for you are not the only one disturbed by distractions. Our mind is extremely flighty; but, since our will is mistress of all our powers, it must recall the mind and carry it to God, as its last end.

When the spirit, which has not been subdued in the beginning, has contracted some bad habits of wandering and dissipation, they are difficult to conquer and ordinarily drag us, in spite of ourselves, to the things of earth.

I think that a remedy for that is to confess our faults and to humble ourselves before God. I do not advise you to talk much at prayer, since long discourse is often an occasion of wandering. In prayer, hold yourself before God like a poor dumb man and a paralytic at the door of a rich man, and occupy yourself in keeping your soul in the presence of the Lord. If it wanders and withdraws from Him at times, do not be upset, for troubles of mind serve rather to distract than to recall it; the will must recall it gently. If you persevere in this way, God will have pity on you.

One means of recalling the mind easily during the time of prayer and of keeping it more in repose is, not to let it make much effort during the day, but to hold it exactly in the presence of God. Being accustomed to remind yourself of Him from time to time, you will find it easy to remain tranquil during your prayers, or at least to recall your mind from its wanderings.

I have spoken to you amply in my other letters of the advantages that can be derived from this practice of the presence of God. Let us busy ourselves with it seriously and pray for one another. I recommend myself also to the prayers of Sister ———— and of Reverend Mother————.

NINTH LETTER

(To the Same)

March 28, 1689

Here is the answer to the letter I received from good Sister————; please give it to her. She seems to me full of good will, but she wants to go faster than grace. One does not become holy all of a sudden. I commend her to you, for we must help one another by our advice and still more by our good example. You would do me a favor by giving me news of her from time to time, whether she is very fervent and very obedient.

Let us often reflect, my dear Mother, that our sole occupation in this life is to please God. What can all the rest be, save folly and vanity? We have passed more than forty years in religion; have we used them to love and serve God, Who by His mercy had called us for that purpose? I am filled with shame and confusion when I reflect, on the one side upon the great graces that God has given me and still continues ceaselessly to give me, and on the other, upon the ill usage that I have made of them and my slight profit in the way of perfection.

Since by His mercy He gives us still a little time,

let us begin all over again and repair the lost opportunity. Let us return with entire confidence to this kind Father, Who is always ready to receive us lovingly. Let us renounce, dear Mother, renounce generously for love of Him everything that is not He, for He deserves much more than that. Let us think of Him continually and place all our confidence in Him. I do not doubt that we will very soon experience the effects of this and feel the abundance of His graces, with which we can do everything—and without which we can commit only sin.

We cannot avoid the dangers and reefs of which life is full, without the actual and continual help of God; so let us ask Him for it ceaselessly. How can we ask for it, without being with Him? How can we think of Him often, except by the holy habit of doing so which we must form? You will say that I am always telling you the same thing. It is true, for I do not know any means more fitting or easy than that one; and as I do not practice any other, I advise this one to everybody. We have to know before we can love, and in order to know God we must often think of Him. Even when we do love Him, we will also think of Him very often, for our heart is where our treasure is! Let us think of Him often, and think well.

TENTH LETTER

Paris, October 29, 1689

Madame,

I have had a great deal of difficulty in deciding to write to Mr.————. I do so only because you and Madame de———— wish it. Please be so good as to address and send it. I am well satisfied with the confidence you have in God, and hope that He will increase it for you more and more. We cannot have too much in a Friend so good and so loyal, Who will never fail us, either in this world or in the next.

If Mr.———— is wise enough to profit by his loss and places all his confidence in God, He will soon give him another friend, more powerful and better disposed. God deals with hearts as He will. Perhaps there was too much of the natural in his love and too great an attachment to the one he lost; we should love our friends, but without prejudice to our love of God, Who must be first. Remember, I pray you, what I recommended to you—which is, to think often of God, by day and night, in all your occupations, your exercises, even during your amusements. He is always near you and with you. Do not leave Him alone; you would fear being rude, if you left alone a friend who was visiting

you. Why abandon God and leave Him alone? Do
not forget Him! Think of Him often, adore Him
ceaselessly, live and die with Him. That is the real
business of a Christian; in a word, it is our profession. If we do not know it, we must learn. I will
help you with my prayers.

ELEVENTH LETTER

November 17, 1690

Reverend and honored Mother,

I do not ask of God your deliverance from
pain, but I do beg Him insistently that He may give
you the strength and the patience to suffer them as
long as He pleases. Console yourself with Him Who
holds you attached to the cross, for He will detach
you when He thinks fit. Blessed are they who suffer
with Him. Accustom yourself to suffer in this way,
and ask of Him the strength to suffer as much as
He wishes and as long as He judges it necessary.
The world does not understand these truths, and I
am not surprised at it, for they suffer like people of
the world and not like Christians. They look upon
maladies as pains of nature, and not as graces of
God, and therefore they find in them nothing but
what is contrary and harsh for nature. But those
who consider them as coming from the hand of
God, as effects of His mercy and means that He is

using for their salvation, ordinarily find in them great sweetness and sensible consolation.

I would like you to convince yourself that God is often nearer to us in seasons of illness and infirmity than when we enjoy perfect health. Seek no other doctor than Him. As far as I can understand the matter, He wishes to heal you Himself. Place all your confidence in Him; you will soon see the results, which we often delay by having greater confidence in medicines than in God.

Whatever remedies you use, they will act only in so far as He permits. When the pains come from God, He alone can heal them; He often leaves us ills of the body to heal those of the soul. Console yourself with the sovereign Physician of souls and bodies.

I foresee that you will tell me that I am having an easy time of it, that I eat and drink at the table of the Lord. You are right. But do you think it would be a small embarrassment to the greatest criminal in the world to eat at the table of the King, to be served by his hands, without being assured of his pardon? I think he would feel a very great trouble, which only confidence in the goodness of his Sovereign could moderate! So I can assure you that, whatever sweetness I feel in drinking and eating at the table of my King, my sins, forever present before my eyes, as well as the uncertainty of my pardon, torment me; although, in truth, the pain is agreeable to me.

Content yourself with the state in which God has placed you: however happy you believe me to be, I envy you. Sorrows and suffering will be to me a paradise when I suffer with God, and the greatest pleasures would be a hell to me, if I tasted them without Him; my whole consolation would be to suffer something for Him.

I am very close to the point of going to see God, I mean, going to render an account to Him. For if I had seen God one single moment, the pains of purgatory would be sweet to me, even should they last until the end of the world. What consoles me in this life is, that I see God by faith; and I see Him in a manner which might sometimes make me say: "I no longer believe, but I see, I experience what faith teaches us." On this assurance and this practice of faith, I will live and die with Him.

Keep yourself, then, always with God, for that is the sole and only solace for your ills; I will pray Him to keep you company. I greet the Reverend Mother Prioress, I recommend myself to her holy prayers, to those of the holy community and to your own.

TWELFTH LETTER

Dear Reverend Mother:

Since you desire with such earnestness that I inform you of the method that I have used to arrive at this state of the presence of God, in which Our Lord, by His mercy, has deigned to place me, I cannot conceal from you that it is with much reluctance that I yield to your importunity, on condition that you show my letter to no one. If I knew that you would let it be seen, all the desire that I have for your perfection would not be capable of inducing me to do it. Here is what I can tell you about the matter.

Having found in several books different methods for going to God and various practices of the spiritual life, I thought that this would serve rather to trouble my soul than to make easy for me what I aspired to and sought after, which was nothing else than a means of belonging wholly to God. This made me resolve to give all for all. Thus, after having given myself entirely to God in satisfaction for my sins, I renounced for His love all that was not He and I began to live as if there were no one but Him and me in the world. Sometimes I considered myself before Him like a poor criminal at the feet of his Judge; other times I regarded Him in my heart as my Father, my God. I adored Him there as often as I could, holding my spirit in His holy presence and recalling it as many times as I found it distracted. I had no little difficulty in this exercise, which I continued despite all the hindrances that I found in it, without being troubled or disquieted when I was involuntarily distracted. I busied myself with it no less during the day than during my prayers; for at all times, at every hour and minute, even in the midst of my work, I banished and drove from my spirit all that was capable of taking from me the thought of God.

That is my ordinary practice, Reverend Mother, since I have been in religion; although I have practiced it only with much cowardice and many imperfections, still I have received from it very great advantages. I know well that it is to the mercy and the goodness of God that they must be attributed, since we can do nothing without Him, and I even less than all others. But when we are faithful to holding ourselves in His holy presence, to considering Him as always before us, besides the fact that this hinders us from offending Him and from doing anything which might displease Him—at least voluntarily—it is by reason of considering Him in this way that we take a holy liberty to ask Him for the graces we need. Finally, by dint of reiterating these acts, we make them more familiar to us and the presence of God becomes a natural thing. Thank Him, if you please, with me, for His great kindness in my regard, which I cannot sufficiently admire for the great number of graces that He has given to a sinner miserable as I am. May He be blessed for everything! Amen.

THIRTEENTH LETTER

November 26, 1690

Dear Reverend Mother,

If we were really accustomed to the exercise of the presence of God, all maladies of the body would seem slight to us. Often God permits that we suffer a little to purify our souls and oblige us to dwell with Him. I cannot understand that a soul which is with God and wants only Him can be capable of pain; I have even enough experience to be sure it cannot.

Take courage. Offer Him your pain without ceasing; ask Him for the strength to endure it. Above all, accustom yourself to converse often with Him, and forget Him as little as you can. Adore Him in your infirmities, offer them to Him from time to time, and in the bitterest of your pains beg Him humbly and lovingly, as a child does of his good father, for conformity to His holy will and the help of His grace. I will help you by my poor weak prayers.

God has many means of drawing us to Him. He hides Himself from us sometimes, but faith alone, which will not fail us at need, must be our support and the foundation of our confidence, which should be wholly in God.

I do not know what God wants to do with me, for I am ever more content. Everybody suffers— and I, who should be doing rigorous penances, feel joys so continual and so great that I have trouble in moderating them.

I would willingly ask God for a share in your sufferings, if I did not know my weakness, which is so great that, if He left me to myself for a moment, I would be the most miserable of all creatures. However, I do not know how He could leave me alone, since faith makes me touch Him with my finger, and since He never departs from us unless we go away first. Let us fear to go from Him, let us be always with Him, let us live and die with Him. Pray to Him for me, and I will for you.

FOURTEENTH LETTER

(To the Same)

My good Mother,

I grieve to see you suffering so long. What sweetens the compassion I have for your pains is, that I am persuaded they are proofs of God's love for you. Regard them in this way and they will be easy for you to bear. My thought is, that you should leave all human remedies and abandon yourself entirely to Divine Providence. Perhaps God is only waiting for this abandonment and a perfect confidence in Him to heal you. Since, in spite of all your care, the remedies do not have the effect they should, but on the contrary the evil grows worse, it would be no longer tempting God to abandon yourself into His hands and expect everything from Him.

I have already told you in my last letter that sometimes He permits the body to suffer in order to heal the illness of our souls. Be brave; make a virtue of necessity. Beg of God, not to be delivered from pains of the body, but strength to suffer courageously for His love all that He wishes and for as long as He pleases.

These prayers are of a truth a little hard on nature, but very pleasing to God and sweet to those who love Him. Love sweetens pain, and when one loves God one suffers for Him with joy and courage. Do it, I pray you. Console yourself with Him Who is the sole remedy for all our ills. He is the Father of the afflicted, always ready to aid us; He loves us infinitely more than we think. Love Him then; do not search any longer for any other solace than in Him, and I hope that you will receive it very soon. Farewell, I will help you in this by my prayers, poor as they are.

*　　*　　*

This morning, Saint Thomas's feast day, I offered Holy Communion for your intention.

FIFTEENTH LETTER

(To the same)

January 22, 1691

My very dear Mother,

I thank God for having relieved you a little as you desired. I have been many times ready to die, although I would never have been so content; moreover, I did not ask for relief, but for courage to suffer bravely, humbly and lovingly. Take courage, my very dear Mother. Oh, how sweet it is to suffer with God! However great the sufferings may be, accept them with love; it is a paradise to suffer and to be with Him. Besides, if we wish to enjoy even in this life the peace of Paradise, we must accustom ourselves to familiar, humble and loving intercourse with Him. We must prevent our mind from wandering, no matter what the occasion may be, for we must make our heart a spiritual temple for Him, in which we adore Him ceaselessly. We must watch over ourselves without relaxing, so as not to do or say or think anything that can displease Him. When we are thus occupied with God, sufferings will be no more than sweetness, unction and consolation.

I know that to arrive at this state the beginning is very difficult and that we must act purely in faith. We know also that we can do everything with the grace of the Lord, and that He does not refuse it to those who ask it insistently. Knock at His door, persevere in knocking; and I promise you that He will open it in His good time, if you do not cease trying, and will give you all of a sudden what He has delayed for many years. Goodbye. Pray to Him for me as I do for you, for I hope to see Him very soon. I am wholly yours in Our Lord.

SIXTEENTH LETTER

(To the Same)

February 6, 1691

God knows very well what we need and all that He does is for our good. If we knew how much He loves us, we would always be ready to receive from His hand with indifference either the sweet or the bitter, and even the most painful and hardest things would be sweet and agreeable to us. The harshest trials ordinarily do not seem unbearable, except through the view we take of them; and when we are convinced that it is the hand of God that is acting upon us, that it is a Father full of love Who places us in states of humiliation, sorrow and suffering, all the bitterness is taken away from them, and our pains have nothing but sweetness.

Let us occupy ourselves entirely in knowing God. The more one knows Him, the more one desires to know Him; and as love is usually measured by knowledge, the greater is the extent and depth of the knowledge, the greater will be the love. If love is great, we will love equally in distress and in consolation.

Let us not stop at seeking or loving God for the sake of the graces that He has given us, however exalted they may be, or for those that He may give us. These favors, great though they are, will never carry us so near to Him as faith does with a simple act. Let us seek Him often through this virtue. He is within us, let us not seek Him elsewhere. Are we not uncivil, and even blameworthy, to leave Him alone, occupying ourselves with a thousand trifles which displease and maybe offend Him? He endures them, but it is much to be feared that some day they will cost us a great deal.

Once for all, let us begin to be His entirely; let us banish from our heart and our soul all that is not He. He wishes to rule alone; let us ask Him for this grace. If we do what we can on our part, we shall soon see within us the change that we are hoping for. I cannot thank Him enough for the little relief He has afforded you. I hope from His mercy the grace to see Him in a few days. Let us pray to Him for one another.